YO-BZA-623

D
790
.K564
1999

Klinkowitz, Jerome.

With the Tigers over
China, 1941-1942.

$25.00

DATE			

BAKER & TAYLOR

With
the Tigers
over China
- • -
1941-1942

With the Tigers over China

- • -

1941-1942

Jerome Klinkowitz

THE UNIVERSITY PRESS OF KENTUCKY

Publication of this volume was made possible in part
by a grant from the National Endowment for the Humanities.

Scholarly publisher for the Commonwealth,
serving Bellarmine College, Berea College, Centre
College of Kentucky, Eastern Kentucky University,
The Filson Club Historical Society, Georgetown College,
Kentucky Historical Society, Kentucky State University,
Morehead State University, Murray State University,
Northern Kentucky University, Transylvania University,
University of Kentucky, University of Louisville,
and Western Kentucky University.

Editorial and Sales Offices: The University Press of Kentucky
663 South Limestone Street, Lexington, Kentucky 40508-4008

03 02 01 00 99   1 2 3 4 5

Library of Congress Cataloging-in-Publication Data

Klinkowitz, Jerome.
  With the Tigers over China, 1941-1942 / Jerome Klinkowitz.
    p.   cm.
  Includes bibliographical references and index.
  ISBN 0-8131-2115-9 (cloth : alk. paper)
  1. World War, 1939-1945—Aerial operations, American. 2. World
War, 1939-1945—Aerial operations, British. 3. World War, 1939-
1945—Campaigns—Pacific Area. 4. World War, 1939-1945—
Personal narratives, American.   I. Title.
D790.K564   1999
940.54'25—dc21   99-13691

This book is printed on acid-free recycled paper
meeting the requirements of the American National Standard
for Permanence of Paper for Printed Library Materials.

Manufactured in the United States of America

For Wendell Lampe and John Lounsberry,
neighbors and friends

Contents

Acknowledgments

− • − *With the Tigers over China* is a study of how participants in America's and Britain's Far East air war during 1941
and 1942 wrote about their experiences. Their writing is particularly important today because this theater of operations
has been too often neglected. It was not a global priority at
the time, and because the nature of its flyers' successes (in an
otherwise losing cause) confounded accepted images of air
combat, it was rarely given its due in official histories afterward. To remedy this situation means reading and considering how the participants viewed their war, something I have
been able to undertake only with the help of many others.

My earlier studies of such materials from the air war in
World War II's European and Mediterranean theaters (*Their
Finest Hours* and *Yanks over Europe*) were aided by firsthand
help from veterans of the conflict, and their personal assis-
tance continues with this book. Therefore, my thanks go to
Leroy Newby (a bombardier on B-24s), Alan F. Kelsey (an
air gunner on Wellingtons and Lancasters), Clyde B. East (a
Mustang pilot), Dr. D.W. McLennan (a flight leader in the
Royal Canadian Air Force), Don Charlwood (a navigator on
Lancasters for the Royal Australian Air Force, serving in
England with the RAF), and John Richards (a Coldstream

Guardsman with a special interest in the air battles above his home in Plymouth). In recent years, my work has been enriched by many conversations with my neighbors, Wendell Lampe and John Lounsberry, who were part of the war at sea and in the air and who have helped me comprehend the conflict's larger dimensions; it is to them that this book is most respectfully dedicated.

Aviation specialist booksellers are another important resource, all of whom have provided help especially tailored to a researcher's needs. Among these are Kenneth Owen, of the Owens Book Centre in Tavistock, England, whose shop near the old corn market contains signature boards from flyers in almost every RAF unit from World War II, including the American Eagle Squadrons. Others are Brian Cocks of Helpston, near Peterborough, and—in the United States—Jim Peters of Crawford-Peters Aeronautica (San Diego) and the specialists at Zenith Aviation Books (Osceola, Wisconsin). Collector and literary critic Peter Reed, an RAF veteran teaching at the University of Minnesota, has been a great help and good friend. Terrence J. Lindell of Wartburg College shared resources, as did Robert F. Donahue of Springfield, Massachusetts, who most kindly supplied photographs found among the effects of his late brother, Flight Lieutenant Arthur G. Donahue, an American volunteer in Britain's Royal Air Force. Bob Nandell of the *Des Moines Register* and independent researcher Tom Boyle of Bennett, Iowa, supplied photographs as well, for which I am grateful. Professionally, the University of Northern Iowa and its Graduate College remain my sole source of research support, most recently a semester's Professional Development Leave. My wife Julie has been a patient companion in exploring old air bases in the United States, England, Europe, and the Pacific. Our family's peacetime flyer, my uncle, Lieutenant Colonel Richard P. Klinkowitz, Wisconsin Air National Guard, Retired, has always been an inspiration, from sitting me in an F-89 Scorpion cockpit as a youngster to discussing military flying in recent years. Most of all, I am grateful to the memoirists themselves, who not only fought an especially dangerous war but wrote about it when it was a less than popular thing to do.

Geographical, Historical, and Textual Notes

– • – Burma, China, and Singapore form the geographic triangle that constitutes the Far East of this book. Once a province of India, by 1940 Burma (to the immediate east of the Indian subcontinent and directly south of China's western reaches) was a separate country, albeit under British control. Located south of both Burma and China at the tip of the Malay Peninsula, Singapore in 1940 was a British crown colony. Although Burma gained independence from British rule in 1948, Singapore remained part of the Commonwealth until 1963.

In the air war fought in Far Eastern skies, the Japanese Zero fighter was a worthy opponent of both the American P-40 Tomahawk and the British Hurricane. Its success prompted an equivalent of the "Spitfire snobbery" prevalent among Luftwaffe pilots in the European Theater, for just as German pilots preferred to identify their troublesome opponents as being R.J. Mitchell's classic warbird, many American and British flyers tended to report any well-performing low-wing monoplane as the Mitsubishi Zero, when in fact the adversary could well have been the Nakajima Ki-43 Hayabusa.

In June 1941, the United States Army Air Corps (USAAC)

was renamed the United States Army Air Force (USAAF), which in 1947 became a separate service, the United States Air Force (USAF). In the narrative that follows, American forces are described by their name at the time and by the appropriate abbreviation.

Publication dates are given at the first appearance of works cited in the text. Thereafter, pagination is given in parentheses. A full bibliography of books quoted is found at the end.

Introduction

— • —

The War that Wasn't First

— • —   No universally common date marks the beginning of the Second World War. Depending on when which of the eventual Allied or Axis powers joined it, its commencement can be years apart. The Soviet Union, for example, was a belligerent only in the European theater until August 1945, when at the very end it declared war against Japan. Italy was in an even more complex position, not declaring war on the Allies until June 1940 and being taken out of the Axis well before Germany surrendered. Britain's declaration in September 1939 and America's entry in December 1941 are more evident dates, provoked as they were by Hitler's assault on Britain's ally Poland and the Japanese attack on Pearl Harbor, respectively.

When it comes to World War II in the Far East, starting times are even more problematic. Is it July 7, 1937, when Japan began a shooting war with China at the Marco Polo Bridge? Or is the real date as early as 1931, when Manchuria was declared a Japanese protectorate? If either date is accepted, it makes the Far Eastern theater the Second World War's first scene of action. Adding credibility to this notion, especially in terms of the air war that so distinguished the entire world conflict, was that one of its major American figures was working on military aviation in China four and one half years before Pearl Harbor. But even if Claire Chennault's employment by Generalissimo Chiang Kai-shek is considered a localized anomaly, his subsequent organization of the American Volunteer Group, or AVG, must count as a serious factor as China and the rest of the Far East became a theater of globally important air combat.

Yet because the men in what became known as the Flying Tigers were a volunteer group, and even more so because hostilities did not come to Britain's territories in the Far East until even later—beginning in December 1941, so long after the Blitz on Poland, the Battle of France, and the Battle of Britain had characterized England's air war as a cross-Channel affair—conflict in the Far East was regarded as the war that wasn't first. Claire Chennault and his AVG personnel certainly felt that way as they struggled with ill-supplied and worn-out equipment, facing a powerful enemy with numbers so paltry as to be laughable. Art Donahue, an American in the Royal Air Force who'd already fought in the Battle of Britain, knew he was similarly outgunned and outnumbered when he and a handful of Hurricane pilots undertook the aerial defense of Singapore. By the time the few other RAF squadrons were routed from Burma in March 1942, history had codified what by this time had become a strategic decision: that even though America's entry into World War II made it a two-ocean conflict, securing the Atlantic and putting the Allies in a position to defeat Germany first had to be priorities. And so they were.

Because it was the war that wasn't first, the air combat that American and British pilots fought in Far Eastern skies during 1941 and 1942 was a vastly different experience from what transpired elsewhere. Some of this had to do with timing, and even more with special geographic and climatic conditions of the region. But most emphatic was the structural difference between the war in Europe and what was happening in Asia. Between September 1939 and May 1940 England and Germany found themselves in an adversarial standoff that pantomimed those that characterized the 1914-18 war. There were no trenches, of course, but parallel lines of opposition prevailed for eight months of the so-called

Phoney War, in which from the fall of Poland to the invasion of France the two major powers stood against one another in a state of war without making moves toward the other's territory. The face-off replicated the chessboard structure of the First World War, one that from Britain's point of view had characterized its last century and a half of orientation toward Europe. As for America's presumed eventual entry, it was visualized just as in World War I, coming in later as active allies to a Britain and France it had previously supported in more tacit fashion.

For both the United States and Great Britain, the Far East was a peripheral factor in its early planning. Both countries had interests in the region and expressed them economically. Because of its system of empire inherited from centuries previous, Britain maintained colonial relationships with India, Burma, Singapore, and Hong Kong. Because this system had been in place for so long and suffered no appreciable external threats to its stability, military presence was not a major factor beyond that of the garrison variety. Following Japan's withdrawal from naval agreements and Britain's termination of the Anglo-Japanese alliance in the years following World War I, it became evident that some defensive enhancement was needed, and in 1921 Singapore was designated as a fortress base for a permanent Far Eastern fleet. The fortress was built but never given the air defense it needed and deserved, while government economies and subsequent international naval treaties made major naval presence an emergency rather than standing condition.

American participation in Far Eastern affairs was much more limited, and as late as the 1930s and even 1941 itself was undertaken less as firm policy than in the adventuresome sense of England's eighteenth-century involvements— a matter not for government leaders and great national institutions to pursue but rather the business of individual companies and colorful adventurers. The difference was that an earlier era's sailing ships had been replaced by airplanes, and it was as an open field for aviation development that the Far East interested Americans. With its important population centers separated by vast distances and having no modern transportation system to speak of, China was a natural place for air-minded persons to turn. Because so many other nations had sent military air missions to China, the United States did, too, under Colonel John H. Jouett in 1932. Here an aviation school was established, the aim being less immediately military than to establish a customer-base for American materials and services. Salesmen soon followed, including William Pawley for the Curtiss-Wright Aircraft Company and Harvey Greenlaw for North American Aviation. Both of these were to be involved in another venture begun by an even more exceptional character, Claire Lee Chennault, who after a frustrating career in the peacetime U.S. Army Air Corps had retired as a captain in 1937 and had immediately gone to work in China as Chiang Kai-shek's chief air advisor. After several failed experiments at improving the Chinese Air Force, including supplementing it with an International Squadron staffed by an odd collection of European and American adventurers, Chennault decided to form a volunteer group of service-trained professionals to defend China from the air. In October 1940, he began approaching both U.S. government officials and British representatives in Washington, D.C., about organizing and supporting the group that would become known as the Flying Tigers. These recruits would have to resign their commissions, remove all insignia from their uniforms, and become employees of a private company doing contract business with the government of China. For a war that wasn't first, this initial agreement for undertaking its air operations was a decidedly unofficial and unconventional affair.

Because of these conditions at its inception, understanding how the air war was fought in this theater of operations could be difficult. Like the war in Vietnam that developed a generation later, few structures from previous armed conflicts applied—certainly none of the official ones, because the first shots fired in the air over China and then Burma came from a force that wasn't officially there. Even when the transition to regular forces was made, matters did not become much easier, because the old irregular commander was still in charge. The fact that his methods had succeeded and continued to do so did not impress the officers of the USAAF he now rejoined (as a general, no less), for they represented a theory of air war that the service had rejected during two decades of peace and which had been "proven" only by a renegade in charge of a small band of ill-behaving mercenaries. During 1943 and 1944 conducting operations became no easier for Chennault; from theater headquarters in India his old rival Clayton Bissell frustrated attempts to get proper supplies, while the overall commander, General Joseph Stilwell, disagreed with both Chennault's tactics for the air war and his close alliance with Chiang Kai-shek.

It was no accident that General Claire Chennault was excluded from surrender ceremonies on board the USS *Missouri* at war's end. He had succeeded by working against accepted practices rather than cooperating with them, and this was a time to signify the end of disorder rather than acknowledge or much less celebrate it. From the British side there was similar, if less explicit, discomfort with how the Far Eastern air war fit in the larger scheme of things: the fall of Burma remained an embarrassment and Singapore's capitulation a major disgrace, while the RAF had repurchased respect only by changing its mission radically from a supposedly indomitable defensive force to a new style of warfare excelling in ground support and long-range air supply. Neither country's conduct in the region, whether in losing ground initially or regaining it in the long run, conformed with the larger image promulgated in the more prominent European theater. There, defense had been heroic and offense carried through with the smashing weight of great four-engine-bomber fleets, as if seeking to confirm prewar military thinking that "the bomber will always get through." In China it had been a Japanese bomber force that Claire Chennault's ragtag fighters had defeated, while in its subsequent operations from India the RAF's four-engine force of Liberator bombers carried far more parachutists on clandestine operations than they did explosives. Covert operations, successful as they may be, are rarely given contemporaneous recognition with medals, commendations, and news stories. As for the American Volunteer Group's work, it was likewise off the record; its flyers received no U.S. decorations, no record for their AVG kills in postwar victory totals, and no credit for their service time with Chennault's outfit.

Therefore, official histories are not the place to look for complete and compelling accounts of the war that wasn't first. But a great number of personal narratives exist, from General Chennault's autobiography to the memoirs of his unranked pilots and technicians and the stories written by flying officers and wing commanders who served in RAF units during those first Far East air combats from December 1941 through March 1942. Here can be read much fuller and more accurate accounts of what transpired during this crucial period so atypical of the larger conflict. It is not unusual for an individual veteran to read an accepted version of events in which he or she participated and remark that no, things were not really like that at all. For what happened in the Far East at this time, such distinctions carry larger importance, for what the individual experienced is more likely not to have fit the official version of events. How, for example, can British strategists admit that a lowly flying officer such as Terence Kelly might be right in saying Singapore, Sumatra, Java, and even Burma could have been held by the forces available, if only people such as those who wrote the official histories had used them right? And how can the leadership of the USAAF give proper credit to a leader such as Claire Chennault, who fought the Army Air Corps through two terms of service and from two periods of retirement?

When it comes to individual stories, the very reasons their actions do not fit well with the official picture make them all the more valuable as narratives. Consider wing commander Bunny Stone, an RAF officer who distinguished himself from his colleagues by taking the officially scorned AVG advice on tactics and even more so by cozying up to these egregious renegades. Within the AVG itself, colorful characters abound. Well beyond Chennault himself and his frankly outspoken manner was Greg "Pappy" Boyington, who raised hell with the Volunteers and went on to lead his own Black Sheep Squadron in Marine aviation along the same lines as his old boss used with the AVG. There was the group diarist and wife of Chennault's chief of staff, Olga Greenlaw, whose *The Lady and the Tigers* reads as one of the most remarkable memoirs from any operational theater—so remarkable that it took her reputed lover, Pappy Boyington, two books of his own to deal with the world she described, *Baa Baa Black Sheep* and *Tonya*. Even the AVG's chaplain, Paul Frillmann, was colorful enough to publish a commercially successful memoir, detailing not only his work with Chennault but a subsequent career with the CIA. As far as engaging in spook work, Frillmann was not the only AVG alumnus to do so. Gerhard Neumann was a German national working in Hong Kong when the war broke out. After fleeing inland, he hooked up with Chennault as a chief mechanic, rebuilding a crashed Zero to flyability and after the war driving a Jeep all the way to Jordan before working with the Office of Strategic Services and going on to direct jet engine development for the General Electric Corporation. Erik Shilling, qualified as the AVG's best reconnaissance pilot, stayed with his boss through postwar Civil Air Transport (CAT) days and, in this capacity, flew covertly supplied American C-119s in support of the French troops besieged in 1954 at Dien Bien Phu. CAT itself later became the CIA's private airline, Air America, making the longer story resulting from AVG roots even less of an officially accountable affair. Nor had the AVG's replacement on July 4, 1942, by the USAAF's 23rd Fighter Group brought an end to the monkey business and color, for the group's first commander had an interesting history of his own and told it in a series of best-selling books from 1943 to 1988. Robert Lee Scott Jr. was an aviator after Chennault's own heart, fighting his way into combat service and even then acting well beyond official channels to begin freelancing with the AVG in the months before its scheduled retirement. American adventuring had made its way into the RAF as well. Not only did AVG pilots fly alongside their British counterparts in defense of Rangoon, but one of the handful of pilots on hand for the last days of Singapore was Art Donahue, a volunteer in the RAF from a farm near St. Charles, Minnesota. Like almost every other person involved in the Far East's air war at the time, he was operating considerably out of conventional bounds.

This rich literary record is inscribed within the time limits necessary for any analysis to make sense. The American Volunteer Group was organized on paper in the early months of 1941, with the United States letting one hundred of its pilots resign their service commissions and two hundred of its ground crew and technicians out of their enlistments in order to join Chennault's project. As the first of three contingents of these men (and two women serving as nurses) made plans to sail the Pacific in the summer 1941, the RAF (which had earlier considered supplying veteran flight leaders and squadron commanders) agreed to turn over an airfield at Kyedaw, outside the city of Toungoo in Burma, as a training facility. Destined for active duty in China, the AVG had to answer an emergency first, helping defend Rangoon from Japanese air attacks beginning December 23, 1941. By this time, the RAF was standing alone against Japanese bombers in Singapore, where attacks had begun almost simultaneously with the action against America's fleet at Pearl Harbor. By mid-February Singapore had been surrendered and the withdrawing RAF squadrons were on their way out of Sumatra as well. Japanese forces landed in Java on March 1, while ever since the fall of Singapore their air fleets had been directed in greater numbers against Rangoon. That city was evacuated early in March and was taken by the Japanese on the eighth of that month. Meanwhile, AVG squadrons had flown to Kunming, China, while their ground units retreated up the Burma Road. Some RAF personnel who had become friendly with the AVG wished to continue fighting against the Japanese advance in northern Burma with their American counterparts, but British plans dictated a withdrawal to India, where as early as April 1 these remnants reformed as 224 Group in order to continue a much different style of air war. From China the AVG fought on until July 4, 1942, when after an unsettled period of internal dissension and controversy over whether it would be taken into the United States Army Air Force (which had recommissioned its leader Claire Chennault as a general) the original mercenary corporation was dissolved, most of its personnel allowed to return home, and regulars from the USAAF took over duties as the 23rd Fighter Group.

At the outside, then, the war that wasn't first covered almost exactly one year, with British action and the toughest American air fighting taking little more than three months. But the activities packed into this period rival that of any single chapter in the larger story of how World War II's air combat was written. And what a literary treasure it is. From Claire Chennault fighting the Japanese on one hand and his own superiors on the other to pilot Erik Shilling crash landing on a primitive people's hillside and wondering if he were to be eaten alive, the story is a rich one. Some of it, like Chennault's studied and editorially assisted biography, is crafted with the care given to a great document in history. Other parts, such as Shilling's memoir, self-published to satisfy the interests of his small-town California airport buddies of the 1990s, draw their appeal precisely from such informal candor. Some of the flyers were already professionals at the writing game: Kenneth Hemingway was an English journalist with a book on factory conditions already to his credit, Barry Sutton had done a book on his Battle of France and Battle of Britain exploits, and Art Donahue was already known in both England and America as the author of *Tally Ho! Yankee in a Spitfire*, the first such tale of an American in the RAF. That these three pilots knew their way with pens and typewriters as well as with Hurricanes and Spitfires made the literary record all the better, just as Terence Kelly's latent talents as a playwright (developing in postwar years) make his three books about the Far East air war all the more digestible.

By the end of 1941, thanks to an American news media starved for good war news, Claire Chennault became a widely known figure. Before the war's end, Robert L. Scott did the same for himself thanks to his best-selling books, one of which (*God Is My Co-Pilot*) was also produced as popular film. In the 1950s and 1960s, it was Pappy Boyington's turn, with a memoir that formed the basis for a television series, *Baa Baa Black Sheep*. A generation later it was time for more figures to be heard, as well, from pilots to crew chiefs, radio operators, a group diarist, the unit's chaplain, and others, from Americans and Germans and Chinese to Englishmen and Australians. For them, the war that wasn't first remains a priority in their lives, providing a lesson to be learned today about making first things first.

Tigers over Burma

– • – None of it was meant to happen as it did. The individuals recruited for pay and adventure by retired Army Air Corps captain Claire Lee Chennault were supposed to fly in China, not Burma; their ninety-nine Curtiss P-40C fighters were intended to be just the escort for a larger bomber force that would take Japan out of World War II, perhaps preemptively. These planes were painted not as tigers but as sharks, and even this enfiguration—triangular teeth circling the engine's air scoop and red-pupiled eye set just ahead of its exhaust ports—did not emerge from local circumstance but was borrowed from newsmagazine photographs of similarly decorated Messerschmitt 110s and Royal Air Force Tomahawks from the Battle of Britain and the desert war, respectively. Chennault's men were the "American Volunteer Force," or AVG. It was the Chinese press that called them "Flying Tigers," an appellation they took note of only after it had been picked up back home, complete with a logo professionally designed by the Walt Disney Studios. The name itself did not become an issue until after the AVG disbanded and the label was transferred to successive United States Army Air Force units operating not as volunteers but as regulars in China through the war's end.

The AVG's shift in mission from China to Burma reflects the acceleration of Japan's military aggression beyond the pace Claire Chennault foresaw. By the summer of 1941, China had already been at war with Japan for four long years, driven back from its ocean ports far inland to the relocated capital at Chungking. Here the Japanese proposed to bomb their virtually defenseless victims until a total Chinese surrender was inevitable. Chennault's volunteer force was organized to defend Generalissimo Chiang Kai-shek's people against these aerial attacks. But delays in getting U.S. government approval to recruit from its military forces and holdups in shipping planes disrupted plans for training during fair weather in Kunming. As a result, the AVG had to be grouped at a borrowed RAF air base in Burma, where paved runways allowed operations during the monsoon.

Here, in circumstances far different than they had imagined, the one hundred pilots and two hundred support staff fresh from the United States undertook preparations for an air war that would depart even farther from expectations. But as things would happen, they were fortuitously in the right place at the right time. Japan's occupation of French Indo-China had closed off Chiang's last access to the sea; henceforth, he would have to obtain desperately needed supplies by rail through Burma and thence via the Burma Road to his territory. Only air power could defend this route from attack, and the AVG had the only effective air forces available. Yet just as they completed their training and began combat operations, the volunteers had to cope with an even more immediate enemy move. On December 23, 1941, Japanese forces began heavy aerial bombing of Rangoon. Because resident RAF squadrons were ill equipped and drastically outnumbered, AVG assistance was requested and given in the form of one squadron being sent into the fray. Together, the newly allied forces beat back the aerial aggressors by inflicting casualties too massive for sustainable offense. The larger results were even more encouraging: by settling the first real losses on Japan, Chennault's flyers had given the United States its only bit of good news since the disasters at Pearl Harbor and Wake Island earlier in the month. From this first major engagement with the enemy, the Flying Tigers legend would begin.

Yet that legend was born from conditions far different than any of its participants had foreseen. Fighting in Burma rather than China, the AVG was in radically alien surroundings. Exotically foreign as it was, China had benefited from American aviation for a decade. During the 1930s, as the country emerged from an era of warlords and banditry to its first form of modern political leadership under Chiang Kai-shek, this once-remote country became an adventure ground and a source of opportunity for pioneer flyers. Russians were there, as were Italians; an American mission arrived in 1932, quite romantically so as one of its pilots was the son of Christy Mathewson, famous pitcher for the old-time New York Giants. Commercial pilots, as well, had a world open to them, where vast distances and lack of conventional transportation made what aircraft could do all the more valuable. Militarily and commercially, China was the new air frontier. Pilots, if they hadn't been there themselves, had been hearing about it for years. Now, in the summer of 1941, it appeared as a way to fight for an ally's freedom and get in on the ground floor of the new war. No wonder so many hotshot pilots of the peacetime Air Corps, Navy, and Marines wanted to head to this part of the Far East.

If China represented a land and people prospectively within the American orbit, Burma was most definitely not. Here was no potential new ally in trade and development, but a culture long subjugated to the supply of raw material (lumber, oil, tea) and serving as the military outpost of conquerors who had won dominance a century before. Issues of empire and colonialism were evident in every facet of Burmese life. As in China, there was a movement toward modernism and independence—but by virtue of their role in supporting British power the AVG was on the opposite side of it.

Apart from the alien style of colonialism, Chennault's pilots found themselves in an uncomfortable environment. Known from Battle of Britain lore as tough and resilient, the Royal Air Force establishment in Burma and the rest of the

Far East was dispirited and soft. Far from the European battle, these elements had continued in the manner of peacetime service in the tropics, where the drill consisted of pink gins, polo, club life, and disavowal that war might ever come. If it did, the putative Japanese enemies were presumed to be as inferior as the native locals their grandfathers had subdued. Not that being wary of danger did any good, for any requests to have their forces strengthened drew only disclaimers from London that back home the mother country was fighting for life, able to spare little or nothing.

The AVG's contribution was thus welcomed, but not the manner of it. Even in wartime conditions their rough manners and lusty bravado would have grated against British dispositions; in a colonial post long used to the pleasures of peace, the effect was deleterious. To make matters worse, the British were unable to match their own elevated style with power and performance in the air. Their forces were obsolete and undermanned, their strategies for defense almost nonexistent. When war came, as so many refused to admit that it could, the results from Hong Kong and Singapore to eventually Burma itself were a series of ignominious defeats, the only cheers coming from native inhabitants rallying to their hated occupier's departure. This judgment is evident in the titles of the two major British histories of the Far East air campaign, Henry Probert's *The Forgotten Air Force* (1995) and Christopher Shores, Brian Cull, and Yasuho Izawa's *Bloody Shambles* (1992).

Thus, the iconography of air warfare was terribly out of balance for these American flyers cast suddenly into the first rumblings of Britain's loss of empire. As recruits to a China eager for their services, they had been promised lavish accommodation and adulation from a grateful people. That would come in time, once they were established in Kunming. But for the start of their adventurers' experience, conditions were miserable, and local attitudes were not supportive—critical from the British, sometimes hostile from the natives. With the United States brought into the war by Japan's sneak attack on Pearl Harbor, they could feel vindication at their foresight and pride in their role at delivering the first effective return blows. But much of this was overshadowed by the fact that they were located more squarely within someone else's fight—a fight these people, whose country had already been at war for over two years, should have known was coming.

As it happened, there was more than enough heroism on the British side. With inferior equipment and poor direction, the pilots of the RAF's Rangoon squadrons, flying hopelessly inadequate Brewster Buffalo fighters cast off by America years before as almost useless for modern combat, helped repel the first Japanese attacks. Then, using Hurricanes that had been replaced at home by the better performing Spitfire, additional forces delayed the enemy advance through Burma until withdrawal to India could be effected. From India the RAF rebuilt its forces and prepared the long campaign to retake in three years what had been lost in three brutal months. By July 4, 1942, the American Air Force was establishing itself in India as well, besides sending the 23rd Fighter Group to replace the ragtag AVG being disbanded in China that day.

Yet even with the military might of the United States on hand, the AVG's help was still needed. To facilitate the handover, Claire Chennault hoped some of his volunteers would volunteer again for an extra two weeks, lest the Japanese take quick advantage of the new rookie force. Nineteen pilots and thirty-six ground crewmen agreed, even though their year's hard service made them eager for home and despite the fact that the USAAF had been extremely difficult in dealing with them over matters of subsequent enlistment. As bad luck would have it, two pilots died during this fortnight of extra service, including one who had recently married the squadron nurse. So even the AVG's exit from World War II was flawed by mischance.

The most basic circumstances made it inevitable that American experience in China and the Far East would be different from the norms of aerial adventure and warfare. In terms of World War II itself, Japan's entry as an aggressor reshuffled the deck. Chennault's flyers were not the only personnel to be repositioned. The RAF squadrons that in

December 1941 and January 1942 had to be sent so hurriedly to Singapore and Rangoon were diverted en route from previous assignments to the Middle East and Russia; one flight of Hurricanes landed and was rushed into combat still encumbered by its long range auxiliary fuel tanks and desert warfare air filters. Already vulnerable because of their weak positions and thin resources, American and British forces suffered all the more from the first joint Allied decision made after Pearl Harbor: that strategic policy would be directed toward defeating Germany first. Quite practical military, political, and economic realities supported this approach. But underlying it was the unspoken assumption that from both British and American points of view Japan's theater of operations was the Orient, so alien to Occidental interests. Anglo-Saxon attitudes of the United Kingdom looked to Europe for their definitions, if only by contemporary contrast. And in the United States, citizens could identify with combat taking place in countries from which their close ancestors had emigrated and whose culture they still in part shared. Japan's ambitions were in another world, indeed.

How different was the Orient is clear from the way most Americans knew about the doings of pilots and their aircraft in these lands of the distant Far East: not from newsreels and certainly not in the stirring speeches of an embattled Prime Minister from the House of Commons in Westminster that was itself a target for Nazi bombs, but rather from comic strips that exaggerated what already seemed exotic. The earliest narrative record of an American's experience flying in China is by Royal Leonard. His *I Flew for China* (1942) details his experiences dating back to 1935, when he left the United States for a thousand-dollar-a-month job piloting a Boeing 247 airliner for Chang Hsueh-Liang, a warlord known as "the YoungMarshal" who would eventually yield to Chiang Kai-shek. Among the colorful characters he meets among the scores of fellow Americans adventuring in this new land of opportunity is Frank Higgs, already famous as the figure "One-Eyebrow Higgs" in the comic strip *Terry and the Pirates* drawn by Milton Caniff. Leonard's reference (p. 248) would be a singularly familiar point to American readers just then learning about such strange new people as Claire Chennault, the Generalissimo, Madame Chiang, and their curious activities so far from home. Leonard and Higgs wound up flying DC-2s and -3s for the Chinese National Aviation Corporation, in the course of which they met another adventurer, Olga Greenlaw, who as the wife of Chennault's chief of staff and herself the AVG's diarist wrote *The Lady and the Tigers*, a memoir as colorful as the real life comic book characters she described (1943, p. 98).

Even the AVG pilots could not resist experiencing the Far East in comic strip terms, as happens at a crucial point in Erik Shilling's *Destiny: A Flying Tiger's Rendezvous with Fate* (1993). When bad weather forces him to crash land on a wooded mountainside fifty miles short of Kunming, Shilling is not sure how to approach the primitive natives. His most preposterous worry, that the tribesmen will hold him for ransom, is only put to rest when he realizes he's confronting the scene not as an aviator but as a creature captive of his own fantasies. In a footnote to the episode, he tracks things down and also clarifies Higgs's role as a source for more than one character:

> For many years, back in the states, I had been an avid reader of *Terry and the Pirates*. It was a syndicated cartoon strip drawn by Milt Caniff, of exciting adventure stories dealing with the mysterious Orient. It was extremely well drawn, with an intriguing plot. Many scenes depicted in the cartoon were drawn from photographs sent to the artist by Frank Higgs, a close friend and college chum. Frank was a pilot, flying for the China National Aviation Corporation, called CNAC, whom I met later.
>
> During the war, Frank Higgs was portrayed in the cartoon strip as the character *Dude Hennick*, a good looking ladies man. The strip dealt with Chinese warlords, beautiful curvaceous Chinese girls, and river pirates that preyed on the Yangtze River traffic. Reading about the intriguing Orient was very interesting to many Americans, including myself, who read *Terry and the Pirates* religiously. (p. 139)

Milt Caniff's comic strips are as frequently cited in Flying Tiger narratives as are the more lofty Arthurian images that in Battle of Britain literature characterize everything from Churchill's speeches and newspaper accounts to later histories and memoirs. Each style has its own validity for approaching a new situation and making sense of it, and each indicates how the participants saw the nature of their experience: in the Battle of Britain playing out the role of cultural heroes in an epic of millennial proportion, in the Far East being caught up by a fantasy world of danger and intrigue that seemed more appropriate for cartoon characters. In *A Flying Tiger's Diary* (1984), Charles R. Bond Jr. cannot help but call forth such images, even after he has been abroad for over half a year, taking a peek into a high-class Chinese brothel and meeting someone who "reminded me of Miss Lace in the comic strip 'Terry and the Pirates,'" (p. 195), with all the silky curves and exotic stylings Erik Shilling had described. As the American air experience in China continued beyond commercial pioneering and the AVG's adventures to the more stable presence of regular USAAF units, Caniff's cartooning kept pace. Robert Lee Scott Jr., who took over from Chennault's volunteers when they headed home, still could meet plenty of colorful characters, including the combat cameraman Charlie Russhon; as recalled in Scott's *The Day I Owned the Sky* (1988). Russhon's virtually all-dessert diet won him the nickname of "Charlie Vanilla" in Caniff's new *Steve Canyon* comic strip (p. 152). Another Air Force Wing Commander, Casey Vincent, appears in Donald S. Lopez's *Into the Teeth of the Tiger* (1986) not just as one of Chennault's most trusted regulars but as "the prototype for the Terry and the Pirates character, Vince Casey" (p. 213).

As with Battle of Britain lore, reality and myth intertwine, one feeding the other until the result exists in a world apart from both. The best example of the new understanding being forged is that of Bert Christman. In civilian life, this young man had been one of Caniff's illustrators, drawing panels for *Terry and the Pirates* and soon establishing his own strip, *Scorchy Smith,* which followed the adventures of a daredevil aviator working as a mercenary in Latin America. Enlisting as a carrier pilot for the U.S. Navy, Christman—like so many of his colleagues aboard the USS *Ranger* doing affiliation exercises along the Atlantic coast—jumped at the opportunity Chennault's AVG recruiters offered. As quoted in Duane Schultz's *The Maverick War* (1987), Christman "volunteered for China because he thought he could get 'lots of good material for a comic strip out there'" (p. 85). However, no Flying Tigers strip per se resulted, for life itself—and then death—took precedence. Of the twenty-two American pilots who died during their AVG experience, Bert Christman was one of them, shot down on January 23, 1942, when the Japanese resumed bombing Rangoon. In the manner of his death, he reflected both myths and realities that thanks to American newspaper coverage had become as popular as Battle of Britain reports a year and a half before. A handful of AVG P-40s and a few hapless RAF Buffaloes had thrown themselves against a vastly superior Japanese force. Of the sixty bombers attacking Rangoon, Christman and his colleagues scored victories against a reported twenty-one. No matter that postwar records account for only three Japanese losses that day; inflated totals were inevitable in the confusion of combat and welcomed for purposes of morale. How this young pilot died also fits the mythology of war against this newly hated, unchivalrous enemy and in his case can be confirmed by medical evidence. Having bailed out of his bullet-ridden plane, Christman began a parachute descent to safety, at which point he was machine-gunned through the neck.

Claire Chennault was not in a P-40 fighter over Burma that day or any other. Somewhat surprisingly, he never visited his embattled men at Mingaladon airfield outside Rangoon or took part in any offensive or defensive actions elsewhere. Instead, his manner was to direct operations from the AVG's main base, wherever that might be: first at Toungoo, the Burmese air field borrowed from the RAF for training, and later from Kunming within China. Though his accommodations to Chinese strategy might later be questioned, his absence from the fight was never challenged. In January 1942, he was forty-eight years old—a very tough and battered forty-eight, mostly deafened by years of open-cockpit flying and prone to debilitating bronchial afflictions. His role was not of the hands-on leader but rather that of the teacher, the job he'd once had in civilian life and had pursued, to his professional detriment, as an officer in the peacetime Air Corps. Yet in this most unheroic of guises Chennault had come to share the cartoon-like qualities of the AVG life that by this time had begun defining him as an image to the American people. As in the title of his autobiography, *Way of a Fighter* (1949), his style was one of pure aggressiveness, be it against an opponent in the air or behind a desk. For much of his life he seemed to be fighting the forces of history itself—until, as it did in the first months of World War II, history caught up with his vision and proved him at least momentarily right.

If the American Volunteer Group was a colorful outfit, the deep shadings began with its organizer and commanding officer. Taking the AVG to the Far East in 1941 was not the first outlandish thing Claire Lee Chennault did in his lifetime, nor would it be the last. Indeed, the man's entire career was a testament to persistent and sometimes flamboyant independence, almost always directed toward views radically opposed to the conventional wisdom of his times. Tactically, that view privileged fighters over bombers, just the opposite of Air Corps thinking of the 1930s when Chennault was trying to continue his service career. Strategically, his position countered the defense-based orientation within America's isolationist continental limits. Politically, this first of the Flying Tigers was the loosest cannon of all, not only counseling the earliest opposition to Japan's perceived war aims but signing on as no less than a mercenary to help Chiang Kai-shek, at the time Japan's only declared enemy. When after so many years on his own he did get the Tigers organized, it was much more than just another outfit in a war soon assuming global proportions. As Robert Lee Scott Jr. puts it in *Flying Tiger: Chennault of China* (1959):

> He had planned this Volunteer Group as a father plans a family
> of sons to carry on his ideals and his life for him. He had
> dreamed of the tactics he would teach them and had worked
> out every little turn and roll, dive and zoom, spin and maneu-
> ver with almost slide-rule precision before he took them into

the sky. He had prepared for them a decade back, and he could close his eyes now and see each combat formation and what he would do with this group of fighters and what he would do with the [proposed] Second American Volunteer Group, as well as the Third. With such forces he could help his beloved China drive the hated barbarian from their soil and from the sky above it. (p. 23)

Chennault's own character and the nature of his exploits were colorful enough to inspire over two dozen biographies, making him one of the most written-about air leaders of World War II. His penchant for working the press when needed, in such high-visibility venues as *Time* and *Life* magazines, made him the American public's first easily recognized aerial commander—all of this for someone who had retired as a captain in the previous decade and well before the Air Corps had taken him back (as a general, because his eminence demanded no less). Everything about him lent itself to colorful coverage: his highly spiced Louisiana Cajun background, his jauntily gamecock-style disposition and rugged good looks, profile chiseled in granite and face deeply weathered by open cockpit flying. Even his partial deafness added to the appeal. Say something in his presence and one would get a stare as if being deeply questioned and subject to no small suspicion. The man looked every bit the peregrine falcon and lived out this role as well.

Before World War I he'd been a country school teacher, where whipping recalcitrant country boys into shape was as much a part of his duties as professing the three R's (his solution to burning off excess energy was to organize the youths into baseball teams with himself as captain and pitcher). When war came, his application for flight training was rejected, but as a stateside infantry lieutenant he wrangled unofficial flying lessons at Kelly Field. With eighty such hours under his belt he finally won a transfer to the aviation cadet program, but too late to fly in the war. Out of the service for less than three months, he reenlisted as a regular and began a career in fighters: flying, commanding, teaching, and writing, all in a United States Army Air Corps that had been won over by General Billy Mitchell's championing of the bomber and that was unwilling to see this new basis of interservice power challenged.

In several respects, the Depression-era Air Corps was right. Increasing speed, weight, and armament made the dogfighting world of those agile but flimsy World War I fighters a thing of the past. Likewise, the high altitudes and great speeds at which modern bombers could operate would seem to put them beyond reach of single-engine pursuit planes stationed near potential targets. Here Chennault's ideas anticipated what would become the type of organization that defined World War II as it was fought in the air. As early as 1920, when he first learned the era's tactics from aces such as Frank Hunter and Carl Spaatz, Chennault saw little value in the old-fashioned dogfight. Later, when he organized an Air Corps aerobatics team for demonstrations on the barnstorming circuit, he appreciated all the more how fighters operated best not in groups or formations but as fast-striking pairs. As for reaching the bombers' high altitude in time to defend their targets, fighters needed advance warning, something impossible on site but obtainable if some type of early warning network could be arranged. Although its best success would have to wait, for radar was developed just in time for the Battle of Britain, technology as simple as an outlying network of ground spotters with telephones or radios could alert fighters in time to gain altitude from their base. Once positioned above, these forces could be directed against the oncoming enemy by a ground controller, himself filtering and digesting the various pieces of information. Rather than engage aggressive aircraft in prolonged fights, Chennault's defenders could strike quickly from on high before diving away to regain altitude for another hit-and-run pass with one fighter watching out for the other.

This would become the way most of World War II's air battles were fought, and the RAF's organization of early warning, ground controlled interception, and individual or paired fighters swooping in for their attacks allowed for amazing success with minimal resources against intimidating odds in the summer of 1940. Churchill was correct in extolling the exploits of "the few," but the key to their success was the manner of organization. Claire Chennault had foreseen the necessity and devised its essentials of design. Even results in service war games during the 1920s and 1930s proved the system's practical success. But Air Corps politics were slanted the other way, and regardless of how well this captain's ideas worked on paper and in practice they were not to be given any serious attention. Having made little progress in his military career and with even dimmer prospects for the future, Chennault retired on April 30, 1937.

Nevertheless, his career as an innovator and leader in military aviation was far from over, for Chennault's retirement was taken in view of an interesting new possibility. The last performance of his aerobatic unit, the famous "Three Men on a Flying Trapeze," was at the All-American Air Races in Miami, Florida, during December 1935. In attendance were Colonel Mao Pang-chu of the Chinese Air Force and an American businessman, William Pawley, who was selling Curtiss-Wright fighters and helping Mao recruit American flight instructors to teach the Chinese how to fly them. Chennault's partners, Sergeants Luke Williamson and Billy McDonald, had been frustrated at Air Corps prejudice against their status as noncommissioned officers and hence jumped at the chance when General Mao offered them lucrative jobs. Through the coming year McDonald kept in touch, and when his boss—a former U.S. officer and military attaché—died, he was eager to recommend Chennault as the Chinese Air Force's chief air adviser. Salary was the same comparatively astronomical thousand dollars per month that Royal Leonard was earning as a warlord's personal pilot. Chennault's employer, Generalissimo Chiang Kai-shek, was even more eminent as the emergent leader of modern China and was soon to become a major player in world politics, especially politics that included the United States. With Chennault, whom he elevated three ranks to become a full colonel, Chiang's importance in the evolving importance of military aviation was assured.

At the beginning of his China service, just months before Japan's all-out warfare against Chiang's state would mark what some historians consider the real start of World

War II, Claire Lee Chennault could responsibly consider himself a self-invented man. Dedicated as a flyer, he hadn't been wanted by the Air Corps, necessitating a back door entrance through the infantry. Once in, he and his ideas, boldly revolutionary yet accurately insightful as they were, suffered rejection to the extent that, by age forty-three, he might well have been considered a failure, service in his chosen profession having come to an undistinguished end. Now as the world began organizing itself for a level of conflict unknown before and most likely impossible ever since, this pioneer of fighter tactics was about to be given a real-life laboratory in which to perfect his experimental method.

It was China's weakness that made Chennault's laboratory experiment so necessary. By the end of 1937, the poorly trained and weakly equipped Chinese Air Force had ceased to exist as a meaningful fighting force. In 1938 Chennault tried forming a mercenary International Squadron, using the lure of big money ($500 per month salary with a $1,000 bonus for each enemy plane shot down), but his motley group of adventurers from the United States, Germany, France, and Holland proved so dissolute and unmanageable that he had to disband them after their own loose talk among spies led to their undispersed aircraft being destroyed on the ground. The experience, wild and unruly as it was, taught Chennault that he needed the training and discipline of regular military flyers for his ideas to work. By 1939 and 1940, with its back to the wall, Chiang's government was actively seeking American support; Soong Tse-ven, Madame Chiang's brother and already a Washington, D.C., intimate known as "T.V." to insiders, was lobbying the Roosevelt administration for aid. It was here that Chennault would get involved. If the United States would sell military aircraft to China, why couldn't they sell pilots to fly them as well—or at least allow American pilots to sell themselves? By December 1940 a plan was made to purchase five hundred American planes, many of them the latest B-17 bombers, and have this virtual air force flown by American crews detached from regular duties as volunteers for China. Strategy called for the retaking of Chinese bases from which Japan itself would be bombed—preemptively, from an American point of view that found its chief advocates in presidential legal counsel Tommy Corcoran (who viewed Chennault as a Sir Francis Drake to Roosevelt's Queen Elizabeth, privateering for self and country) and Treasury Secretary Henry Morganthau (who considered the firebombing of Japan's wood and paper cities more economically advantageous than facing her air and naval forces in years to come). FDR himself believed that such a move could be achieved by China's agency, with U.S. neutrality preserved. His Secretaries of War and of the Army did not, and when Chief of Staff George Marshall and Air Corps chief Henry "Hap" Arnold insisted that any B-17s available should be saved for Britain, Chennault's rather fantastical plan of wiping out the Japanese Empire with his own private air force came to naught.

Instead, less as a grand strategy than as a symbolic gesture to sooth the China lobby, a hundred P-40B fighters (redesignated P-40Cs after their modifications for overseas service) were sold to Chiang's government, with the promise of more fighters and some light bombers (Lockheed Hudsons) to follow. More important, a presidential order gave Chennault permission to recruit an initial three hundred pilots and ground crew to man these first aircraft. This inaugural recruitment, accomplished through the spring of 1941 and sent to the Far East that summer, was as far as matters got. Crews for Chennault's light bomber force were en route across the Pacific on December 7, 1941, when American entrance into the war caused their diversion to Australia. The Hudson bombers themselves stayed at the factory in Burbank, awaiting assignment to the forces of a now openly belligerent nation. Except for the symbolic Doolittle raid, mainland Japan would not be bombed for years. Even China itself would have to await distractions in Burma before getting full service from Chennault's volunteers. But what an adventure their service would be: for themselves, suddenly freed from the confines of a restrictively peacetime military, and for Chennault himself, who would at last be able to effect his personal vision through command decisions, but most of all for the history of military aviation, which would assume its most modern format almost overnight.

If everything happens for the best, Claire Chennault would rank as one of that sentiment's greatest living proofs. Spurned by the Air Corps and surpassed in both rank and influence by his contemporaries, on the eve of America's participation in World War II he was the only air commander positioned to return blows with any effectiveness against the Japanese; because he was, he became in the early months of 1942 America's first air hero, the only image of post–Pearl Harbor success until Jimmy Doolittle's symbolic force of B-25s used the innovation of carrier launching to bomb Toyko on April 18. Chennault, of course, had wished to do that first and believed he could have ended America's war with Japan before it started. But that would have meant a different, much grander style of warfare than he'd developed on the drawing boards and brought into practice with his three slim squadrons of Flying Tigers. One of the first news media correspondents to cover his work, Eric Sevareid of the Columbia Broadcasting System, assessed Chennault's abilities as much stronger on the side of close tactics, as recalled in *Not So Wild a Dream* (1946):

> I was sharply impressed by this legendary figure, but wondered whether the legend was not more impressive than the figure. He was a man who did not smile easily; he was a little deaf and like many deaf persons gave the impression of being somewhat humorless. With a pointer he showed me on the maps his whole system of triangular defense by interlocking airfields, and I was surprised to find that he had so many alternative locations from which to work. (So, one may add, were the Japanese.) If his opinion of the Chinese was much higher than that of so many other American officers it was not only because they worshipped him almost as a god, but because the secret telephone and short-wave warning system by which they reported enemy planes almost as soon as they took off from Hong Kong really did work. Chennault was a hard driver, and all his men respected him, but except for a few close to him there was no feeling of affection; he did not "inspire" the mass of his men in the Stilwell way. It seemed to me that he was a man who had developed the arts of combat

tactics almost to perfection. But he was a limited technician—not, I thought, a man of expansive imagination, capable of handling the immense strategic and political problems which American officers were contending with in all parts of the world. (p. 332)

A similar view came from Joseph W. Alsop, the popular columnist, Washington insider and Roosevelt family confidant (he was a cousin of Eleanor during a presidential administration in which such connections counted highly), and eventual procurement officer for Chennault's improvised American Volunteer Group staff. In his *"I've Seen the Best of It": Memoirs* (1992), Alsop describes his boss as "something of a military genius" but in the style of "homemade learning of the kind one might have found in one of Andrew Jackson's commanders"—in other words, a tactician in the command of another master not of grand strategy but fiercely close-fought tactics. "Jackson himself must have been the same type of man," Alsop admits: "More flamboyant, less canny, but with the same saltiness and the same daring" (pp. 167-68). Self-taught, salty, daring men successfully command regiments, or their equivalent in military aviation, air groups; they are rarely the leaders of full armies.

It was a composite of the character sketched by these two media geniuses who greeted the first contingent of AVG recruits arriving at the Rangoon docks on July 28, 1941. Paul Frillmann was a former missionary hired by Chennault to be the AVG's chaplain and recreation and local liaison officer, and in *China: The Remembered Life* (1968) he describes the scene as it unfolded when his sometimes boisterous charges for the trans-Pacific journey met the man who would be their leader:

> I don't suppose anyone could have called Chennault "glamorous" to his face without being punched. But he was a vain man, and obviously relished making an impression. Like MacArthur, he had immense natural magnetism on which to base his public figure. That day on the docks he was wearing some slapdash adventurous costume as usual—mosquito boots, officer's shirt with Chinese insignia, beat-up Air Force cap—which emphasized his gamecock look. Watching him for only a few minutes, anyone would get the impression of

informality and lack of military pomp, plus a quick, sure air of decisive authority. I don't think any of the men on our ship had ever seen him before, and as I looked down the rail where they were lined up, staring silently at him, I could see that for the time being anyway, Chennault had them all in his pocket. (pp. 62-63)

First impressions did not necessarily last. Faced with the more-than-disappointing conditions in Burma and still months away from their chance to earn hefty bonuses for downing Japanese planes over China, some AVG men turned sour—resigning to go home or going native to work the lucrative Burmese black market. But as soon as Chennault could institute his training regimen, things changed. "The pilots found Chennault a good teacher," Frillmann notes, "and his information about Japanese planes and tactics was new and fascinating" (p. 70). The leader's autobiography is replete with metaphors from teaching and coaching, his model of organization not that of service life but of the university: "For rigid military discipline I tried to substitute a measure of simple American democratic principles. Rigid discipline was confined to the air and combat matters. On the ground we tried to live as nearly as possible under the circumstances as a normal American community." As a result, he was pleased to see that "the barracks at Kyedaw Field during the training period had much the atmosphere of a college campus on the eve of a homecoming football game" (p. 116). Yet testimony from his pupils characterizes the method as more fatherly than professorial. In *God Is My Co-Pilot* (1943) Robert Lee Scott Jr. finds that the method can be employed via the agency of duck hunting, when the older leader and younger Air Force regular would in fact go through "lessons in tactics, lessons he had learned the hard way against the Japanese" (pp. 219-20), all without Scott thinking they were doing anything else but bagging waterfowl from the Chinese marshes.

It is no exaggeration to say that the Flying Tigers had a lot to learn and that Chennault would have to be careful how to teach it. Royal Leonard sums up the typical American attitude toward the Far East at the start of *I Flew for China*, when his arrival overseas merits this pithy paragraph: "Everything in Shanghai was as I had anticipated. I had seen it all before in the movies" (p. 6). As far as the end result of China service, Leonard's vision is also shaped by images from the movies, this time the destination in a Ronald Coleman movie: *Shangri-La* (p. 113), an actual city his Young Marshal employer planned to build in a temperate mountain valley. Chennault's flyers knew a war needed to be fought and won first, but their mental pictures for it came from the same sources. Russell Whelan's *The Flying Tigers* (1942) uses references to Rudyard Kipling's poetry as an attitude-setting introduction for American readers, and radioman Robert M. Smith thinks of the same poet's work when testing out reality against expectations. Those expectations are an admittedly motivating force, as he explains early in *With Chennault in China: A Flying Tiger's Diary* (1984), remarking on enlistment that "I have always wanted to see more of the world and experience adventure with a big 'A' ever since I read Richard Haliburton's *The Royal Road to Romance*. I would have signed up for $100 a month" (p. 16) as opposed to the $300 plus benefits he was getting. Yet the Burma he's taken to is not exactly Kiplingesque, as he notes soon after arrival: "We spent last night in a Chinese-owned hotel in Mandalay. The town was oriental, dirty and drab. Kipling should have forgotten the name. I think the only reason he used it in his poem was because it rhymed with 'flying fishes play.' The hotel was a hole. It will be better to sleep in the open air on our cots beside the trucks" (p. 32).

Smith had been detached from ground service with the 20th Pursuit Group, United States Army Air Corps, but even a seasoned Naval aviator flying dive bombers off the carrier *Ranger* could be similarly driven, as Duane Schultz explains in *The Maverick War:* "Edward F. Rector was interested in the Far East because of his appreciation of the poems and stories of Rudyard Kipling" (p. 84). Robert T. Smith, the second of three Bob Smiths with the AVG, was an Air Corps instructor at Randolph Field when Chennault's recruiter made contact, and in his *Tale of a Tiger* (1986) he remembers how his childhood reading of Kipling, Joseph Conrad, and

Jack London "did much toward creating a thirst for adventure in far-away places that only increased as the years went by" (p. 31). Hollywood movies are a part of his storehouse of images, too, as drawn on when he views the crew of their coastal steamer about to transport the wary volunteers from Singapore to Rangoon:

> The Captain, First Mate, and Chief Engineer were Norwegians, which was somewhat reassuring. The rest of the crew, perhaps a dozen in number, were a mixture of Malays, Lascars, and Chinese, a crew that could be described as "motley" in the fullest sense of the word. They were about as mean a looking bunch as might have been assembled by Warner Brothers; I had the feeling they'd have been more at home aboard a pirate junk in the South China Sea, and that even Errol Flynn would have had the good sense to say "be my guest" as they drug Olivia De Havilland off, kicking and screaming, to a fate worse than death. (p. 53)

Yet Smith's funniest recollection comes not from the movies but from their pertinence (or lack of it) to real life. "You may not believe this, R.T.," says his squadron mate Bill Reed, who draws him aside after the Lascars and others retire below deck to share a pipe of opium, "but we didn't see a hell of a lot of that sort of thing back in Marion, Iowa" (p. 54), a reminder that whether in fantasy or fact these young flyers are surely strangers in an even stranger land.

Kipling remains the most frequent literary reference in Flying Tiger memoirs. Robert Scott might rue the contrasts these young volunteers were confronting between what they'd read and what they were now encountering, but almost every one of them was grateful for the chance; as Erik Shilling puts it in *Destiny*, "the name Irrawaddy encompassed all the romanticism of the Orient," and now he was meeting this great Burmese river firsthand. "It was well known by those who enjoyed Rudyard Kipling's poems," and even though "Kipling was screwed up on his geography," the AVG pilot, an expert on the lay of the land thanks to his recent photo reconnaissance experience, still understands priorities when it comes to matters of the spirit. "I had read many enchanting poems and stories by Kipling,

AVG veteran Bill Reed from Marion, Iowa, pictured far left with his P-40N in the Chinese-American Composite Wing. (Private collection)

Bill Reed's P-40N after a mishap during takeoff. (Private collection)

and now I was seeing the Far East through his eyes" (p. 80). Such readings help him enjoy the region, unlike many of his colleagues who come to hate it. In a similar manner, Donald Lopez ends his *Into the Teeth of the Tiger* by checking off high points on the three continents and one subcontinent to which his air adventures have taken him, a treasury of wonders anyone would be envious to share. "About the only thing I'd missed," he concludes, "was Kipling's great gray-green, greasy Limpopo River, all set about with fever trees" (p. 236)—an omission that matters less because at least he has the words for it.

The other side of romanticism is evident in Joe Alsop's first view of the Far East, particularly the status of its military aviation. On a supply expedition to Singapore, he's met by the local RAF Squadron Leader, a man "with an enormous mustache who was standing just in front of an open hangar full of aircraft that seemed to have come out of a British boy's book on the First World War." The whole scene is there for him to appreciate: ungainly biplanes with huge engines, none of them with streamlined cowlings, grotesque cylinder heads jutting into the slipstream like ragged spokes on a wheel; guns of a caliber for rabbit hunting; and a network of thin wires knitting their top and bottom wings. "That's one of our fighter squadrons, you know," the somewhat comic figure tells him. "They're a little old fashioned, but they're jolly maneuverable. I think they'll make a good job of it with the Zeros" (p. 176). That Chennault had been submitting freelance intelligence reports on the Zero and other Japanese planes was of no more pertinence to the British than to the Air Corps offices in Washington, where no note was taken. Granted, Japan might well have a powerful navy, modeled as it was on the great British fleet. But an air force, developed all on its own and manned by buck-toothed myopic pilots? There was no way either the RAF or the newly renamed USAAF could take such reports seriously—they must be just more propaganda from the overheated China lobby.

Yet if Washington and London didn't listen to Chennault, his three squadrons of the American Volunteer Group surely would. Part of it was his convincing method. An even larger part was these men's awareness that they were out here, more than halfway around the world, on a very thin string. As Robert M. Smith came to realize, their only hands-on experience with China, much less the even more exotic realms of Burma, Thailand, and Indo-China over which they were flying to start, was the collecting of colorful postage stamps as children. Chennault had been in the Air Corps all the way back to 1918, serving shoulder to shoulder with the men who'd been their own colonels and generals. More impressively, he'd been flying in the Far East since 1937, during almost all of which the air forces under his command had been fighting Japanese aircraft these new men had scarcely heard about.

The first lesson was about the plane they'd fly, the P-40C Tomahawk. The P-40 was first flown in 1938 as an inline-engine modification of the radial-powered P-36 Mohawk, the prototype of which dated back to 1934. Mohawks and Tomahawks were the most widely produced American fighters of their time, but as their nascent era was a time of peace these Curtiss fighters were designed for the country's present isolationist stance: as implements of infantry support and coastal defense. Without superchargers, neither plane was much good above 20,000 feet, which was where so much combat would take place once World War II started. As a result, both planes were relegated to less important theaters: Mohawks to the RAF as it rebuilt two squadrons in 1942 for Burma, and Tomahawks to Chennault's AVG.

What could an AVG pilot do with a heavily armored plane meant to take out tanks, gun emplacements, and naval craft while absorbing fire from the ground? Obviously, he could not engage in dogfights with Japanese adversaries whose own planes sacrificed armor and other defensive weight in favor of quick maneuverability. Given what he had to work with, Chennault was grateful his forces weren't faced with having to defend the United States itself. "It is indeed fortunate that the Battle of Britain in 1940 was not the Battle of America," he observes in *Way of a Fighter*, "for we would have had no Spitfires to win our battle" (p. 24). But even with a backward-looking rather than futuristically designed aircraft, things could be done, especially if weaknesses were turned into strengths (with the opposite being done to the enemy's equipment).

The essence of what the AVG learned from their leader

is reported by pilot George "Pappy" Paxton in historian Daniel Ford's *Flying Tigers: Claire Chennault and the American Volunteer Group* (1991):

> Chennault told us that we had a sorry airplane, as fighters go. That it had two things: diving speed and gunfire. If we used those, we could get by with it. If not, we were going to get shot up, cold turkey.
>
> He told us: never stay in and fight; never try to turn; never try to mix it with them. All we could do was to get altitude and dive on them, or take for granted that the planes you could see were all there were because we would always be outnumbered.
>
> We flew a two-plane formation. Chennault told us to stick with our leader. (p. 78)

The two-plane element was essential for flexibility and quick action—almost as flexible and quick as one fighter operating alone, but without the disadvantage of being attacked from its blind spot below and behind. From his experience with the Air Corps aerobatic team, Chennault knew that two aircraft could work in close coordination; his own stunts involved having three planes tied together with relatively short pieces of ribbon. Observers marveled that the trio performed with the mind of one, which is exactly how the leader had programmed their performance, the number three keying off the action of number two, who was in turn glued to the first plane. Such quickness was mandatory for the turn-around the teacher wanted to achieve, making the Japanese aircraft's agile lightness a detriment and the P-40's cumbersome weight a strong advantage.

In the contest to come, as Chennault saw it, weight could be of use in three ways: for faster dives, for the sturdiness needed to take the stress from quick pull-outs, and for the ability to absorb enemy fire without the pilot being killed or the plane exploding. Two main reasons why the Tomahawk weighed as much as it did were its protective armor and self-sealing fuel tanks. By design, Japanese planes had neither, for any number of reasons: to give their craft superior climbing and maneuverability, in appreciation that it took less time to train a replacement pilot than to build a sophisticated aircraft, and in recognition of the traditional Japa-

Curtiss P-40 Tomahawk fighters in two versions of Flying Tiger livery. (U.S. Army Signal Corps)

nese fighting code that death was better than surviving defeat. AVG hit-and-run tactics would compensate for being outnumbered, while diving from above made weight a speed-building attribute. Altitude advantage had to be won before the engagement started, since it would be impossible to claim once the fight began. No matter what the enemy's numerical superiority, each AVG pilot would be concerned with only one of them at a time, getting in and out of the fray before the larger forces could be organized and directed against him. A highly stressed pull-out, such as the P-40 could handle, would zoom it right back up to altitude for another quick pass. If this did not make the odds equal, it did account for the wildly disproportionate number of Flying Tiger kills to losses. Like the Revolutionary War's Minute Men at Lexington and Concord, Chennault's small force was turning the adversary's greatest strengths into fatal weaknesses, and vice versa. Japan had the strategy, Chennault the tactics, and because his tactics undercut the strategy's chief force, the latter won the day.

Another transformed advantage was concentration of firepower. Here the paired fighters performed their second function, not just covering each other's tails, but once directed to a target, using their guns in tandem. The result, as Chennault's studies and practical experiments had shown, did not simply double the firepower's effect but squared it, giving the effect of four fighters attacking individually rather than of two. This knowledge dated back to World War I and the exploits of German ace Oswald von Boelcke and was part of the doctrine Chennault was angered to see rejected by the postwar air corps, politically committed as it was to the presumed invincibility of the mighty bomber. By 1941, however, the leader's young recruits had been reading about how Britain, so much better equipped than themselves, had been forced to abandon daylight bombing of Germany, because RAF bomber groups were being cut to ribbons by the Luftwaffe and their perfection of the hard-striking yet quickly flexible *rotte*, von Boelcke's key element used anew. What they had been taught in their own service flight schools wasn't working anywhere else in the world, and against the odds they faced straight off in Burma it was obvious that they'd better listen to someone who knew. Having studied Japanese forces firsthand for more than four years and having dedicated his career to the previously rewardless task of devising superior fighter tactics, Chennault had his students' attention.

An important lesson involved a frank appraisal of their own worth. As few as they were, positioned at the long end of American air power in an almost impossible supply situation, and flying an obsolescent fighter no one else seemed to want, the pilots of the AVG might well devalue themselves. When rags had to be wrapped around the hubs of worn out tail wheels, solenoids were improvised from non-standard sources to make their machine guns fire, and Japanese Nates and Oscars flew circles around them when they did get engaged, the Tigers might well decry their weary P-40 Tomahawks as useless. Back home, these planes were not worth much—which was why they were so easily let go. But here in Burma, and even more so to come in China, they were the only effective air instrument available. Hence, every plane, clapped out as it was, became worth more than millions. Pilots were the same. Their high salaries, fantastic bonuses, and relief from confining regulations were testament to that. Their small numbers made them even more precious, for with America's entry into the war so imminent there would not be any more of them as volunteers and not anywhere near enough regulars once the U.S. Army Air Force did move in. As late as March 1943, when Lt. Vernon J. Henderson arrived in China as part of the 16th Fighter Squadron in Chennault's new command, the same pedagogy was still in practice, as Henderson states in Carl Molesworth's *Sharks over China: The 23rd Fighter Group in World War II* (1994):

> As I recall, he not only explained how the P-40s could best be employed against the Japanese fighters, but expressed a broader point of view. Pilots, airplanes, fuel and ammunition were exceptionally precious here at the end of a very long supply line. Conceptually, do all the damage to the enemy you can, but remember there is always another day if you stay alive and your airplane remains flyable. Dead heroes have very little capacity to do further damage to the enemy. Much different from most of the European scenarios, where the "homeland" was involved. Then it was, "Good luck, gentlemen, you are dismissed." (p. 97)

The final component in Chennault's method for using his inferior forces against the Japanese involved an even greater use of flexibility. Just as his planes would attack as pairs rather than in full squadron formation, his three squadrons themselves would never be all in the same place at the same time. Even for the initial Burma conflict, when the RAF was pitiably outnumbered and outgunned and Rangoon lay virtually open to aerial bombardment, he put only one squadron at a time into the city's defense. Another detachment remained further north at Kyedaw Field where they had trained, outside Toungoo, while most strength remained in Kunming, their original Chinese destination and where the AVG had moved once the monsoon period abated in the fall. Here was the first example of a plan that would work to Chennault's advantage not just with the AVG but with the slim assets the USAAF never could improve on even later in the war, given problems of long-range supply and more critical situations elsewhere. "It was this ability to shift my combat operations six hundred and fifty miles in an afternoon and a thousand miles in twenty-four hours that kept the Japanese off balance for four bloody years and prevented them from landing a counterpunch with their numerically superior strength that might easily have put my always meager forces out of business," he would note in *Way of a Fighter* (p. 127). To operate this way meant he'd have to rely on skeletonized resources, pilots sometimes doing their own ground crew work, and with himself and his few close associates functioning as an entire staff. But doing so gave him the swift mobility that made the full potential of air power a reality. Weak as they were, the three squadrons of the AVG made such practice not only possible but absolutely necessary to have a fighting chance against the Japanese.

Thus, Claire Chennault had turned adversity to his benefit, using the counts against him as ways to gain points ahead of the Japanese. In time, his ground crew and pilots began seeing advantages in their battered P-40s as well—perhaps, in the light of unanticipated success, imagining an advantage, but responding in spirit nevertheless. One of the few Flying Tiger memoirists wryly skeptical of the Tomahawk is Greg "Pappy" Boyington. But it is instructive that throughout his iconoclastic *Baa Baa Black Sheep* (1958) he can fault it only in comparison with German and British planes rather than against his Japanese opponents. In each case his source is anecdotal: from North Africa, a story about how a Messerschmitt 109 pilot surprised a P-40 by passing it in a dive and then flashing a victory signal, and from Singapore reports that not only had the RAF's Brewster Buffaloes been chewed up by Zeroes but that "Even the Spitfire had been shot full of holes in trying to turn in dogfights with Japanese fighters" (p. 52). Granted, the Spitfire was vastly superior to the P-40, and if the Zero could best it, any hopes for the Tomahawks were dashed, but there were no Spitfires at Singapore. What Boyington must have heard about was its inferior cousin, the Hurricane. Yet the lesson was well taken, and Pappy, much more vaunted for his recklessness and ill discipline than for his flying prowess at this time, resigned from the AVG before its year abroad was over.

Pilots who stayed, and even the USAAF regulars who replaced them, had more time to see the Curtiss-Wright Tomahawk do well against the Japanese again and again. Eventually a Zero was captured and rebuilt to operational standards, making comparisons easier and with some measure of precision. The work was done by Gerhard Neumann, a German national who had been adventuring in China since 1939. Starting off as an automobile mechanic in Hong Kong, he had fled inland as the war began, signing on with Chennault's forces as a crew chief. After the war's end and some consulting with the Office of Strategic Services, he repaired an Army Jeep and with his wife drove over an almost impassable route from China to Jordan, from whence he flew to the United States and an eventual career with General Electric as director of its jet engine division. In his autobiography *Herman the German* (1984), titled for his Air Force nickname, Neumann confirms this plane's strengths and weaknesses, crediting its equal horsepower at half the weight and understanding its fatal flaw: "The rugged and heavy P-40 could be shot full of holes like a Swiss cheese and still keep on flying. The Zero, in contrast, exploded in a ball of fire when hit by American incendiary and explosive shells from fast-firing .50-caliber machine guns" (p. 91). Bruce Holloway was the Air Force colonel chosen to test Neumann's reconstructed Zero, and in *Sharks over China* Carl Molesworth quotes his report:

> First, I flew alongside a B-25 so official and news cameras
> could get some shots. Then I tested it for climb and high speed

at 10, 15, 20, and 25,000 feet. This airplane is greatly overrated. It is highly maneuverable; the P-40 and P-43 are both much faster, sturdier. After these tests, I had a series of dogfights and acceleration tests with both a P-40 and a P-43. I went along in line formation at 200 mph indicated with the P-40. On signal, we both poured on the coal. For a few seconds we stayed together, then the P-40 pulled away so fast it was thrilling— nothing before has ever assured me so much as to who is going to win the war as comparing the Zero and the P-40. The best short definition I can think of for the Zero is a "cheesebox with an engine." (p. 90)

Holloway's test took place on February 2, 1943, a year and a half since Chennault's ninety-nine Tomahawks arrived on the docks at Rangoon. It would be December 1943, at the end of an especially long year of continuing fierce struggle, before the last of these outworn AVG fighters would leave Army Air Force service.

Understanding what they were supposed to do from their side of things, Chennault's pupils also had to learn what to expect from their adversaries, the Japanese. In China, their leader had seen that Japanese fighter pilots could be tricky, leaving one of their colleagues "foundering in sloppy aerobatics while his mates waited in ambush, generally hiding above in the blinding sun" (*Way of a Fighter*, p. 57). Another ploy was what Americans came to call the "squirrel cage," a formation Pappy Boyington describes in *Baa Baa Black Sheep*. A squadron of Japanese fighters would be encountered making a big lazy loop, revolving like a pet rodent's exercise wheel. As the Americans approached, the Japanese would loosen up and spread out a bit, yet staying in the circle. "Their idea was to suck the P-40s inside this beehive, in hopes that we would turn with them. I became so familiar with this change in the Jap formation when about to be attacked that it made them look like a flock of vultures as they hover over a single spot" (p. 63). Forever the bad boy, Boyington ignored Chennault's advice to avoid such tricks and instead devised a way to stay on top and only work his way down as each enemy fighter was picked off. When strafing ground targets, these same fighters would not use the standard Western method of a flat approach followed by a low-level pass but rather flew a figure eight pattern of shooting at their target from a dive, winging over into a climb, then descending for another attack.

Enemy bomber forces made matters simpler by their tight discipline and generally predictable tactics. When attacked, the formations (almost always of twenty-seven planes each) held closely together; any bomber shot down quickly had its place taken by another. The raids were often telegraphed by the regular appearance of reconnaissance flights exactly the same number of hours in advance of each day's raid. The raids were also systematic; if something worked, it would be repeated as an exact duplicate until it didn't work any longer. Advances, when they came, were made with a ground commando mentality, objectives taken in a rush and then held with great patience until supply lines caught up. If there were consistent weaknesses among the Japanese pilots, Chennault taught, they were limited to bomber crews' habit of lowering their guard after they thought danger had passed and fighter pilots' reluctance to improvise when original plans went wrong. At the time of their first combats with the AVG, Japanese forces had not yet learned the need of dispersing their craft at home bases, making the initial AVG attacks more easily effective. Other than that, Chennault's volunteers had to appreciate that their enemy was well-trained, suitably equipped, and strongly dedicated to their objective, which most immediately meant closing down the Burma Road at its origin.

Much has been made of the Flying Tigers' motivation. When their first successes were reported in late December issues of *Time* and *Life* in 1941, another group of American volunteers viewed their exploits with some skepticism. Almost as many—244, and every one of them a pilot—had enlisted in either the Royal Air Force or Royal Canadian Air Force in 1940-1941 to become members of the three RAF Eagle Squadrons, flying Spitfires in defense of England, tangling with the already well-tested, fantastically successful Luftwaffe, and submitting to full RAF discipline as officers in the King's forces. Even compared to what flyers earned in the United States Army Air Force, their pay was piteously small; and when considering that Chennault's men had increased their Air Force pay seven times over and stood chances of multiplying that by getting fat bonuses for kills, the question of whether the Tigers were mercenaries became an apt one. Some of the Eagles asked it, especially in light of their respective foes. Britain was America's closest ally, united by language, tradition, and very real economic bonds. Her plight at the hands of the Luftwaffe was personally understandable and aroused great sympathy; it was almost as if America itself were being attacked. China, on the other hand, was distant and foreign; even when resident in the United States its people were considered an exotic minority. Except for the widely publicized attack on Nanking and vicious treatment of the population, Japan's war against China was by no means as widely acknowledged as the struggle between Germany and England. To President Roosevelt, Prime Minister Churchill was not just an ally but a valued friend; from the world's remote other side, an almost incomprehensible distance away where even the calendar date was different, Generalissimo Chiang was a pesky nuisance. To make comparisons even more individious, the Flying Tigers were in this first stage not even fighting for the defenseless folk romanticized by the China lobby. Instead, they were at an outpost of British colonialism that even the RAF had characterized as scarcely worth the effort to defend, so thin were its allocated resources. To the Eagle Squadrons, the purpose, glory, and very meaningful sacrifice were in their part of the action, not a world away. They themselves would have given anything to be in American military aviation; nearly all of them had tried and been rejected, either because of peacetime quotas or their own physical or educational deficiencies. To them, the AVG consisted of Air Corps or Navy officers who had thrown their careers away to chase the almighty dollar where neither the United States nor Britain thought it worth serious effort. In such light, the Flying Tigers were mercenaries, indeed.

The memoirist who got to know them best was their chaplain, Paul Frillmann—not that after the heat of battle these flyers confided their secret fears. Evidence from the pilots themselves suggests he was regarded as somewhat of a lush, more interested in caring for the group's liquor stores than for their souls. But he was given other important jobs, the first of which was supervising the initial large group of recruits shipped out from San Francisco and arriving at Rangoon on July 28, 1941. The trip wasn't easy, as accommodations were not the plush luxury the men had expected and no workable system for discipline existed. Having a chaplain in charge only compounded the lack of seriousness. Yet in *China: The Remembered Life*, the former missionary made jackleg staff officer admits there was something here that he could at least try to understand:

> On the long haul from Honolulu to Manila, with the ship creeping westward in beautiful tropical weather, we all got to know one another better. I liked nearly everybody, but a pattern was clear. Most men were escaping from frustrations or disappointments, as perhaps I was. They hoped an unknown future in unknown places would somehow give them a second chance. One of the oldest was a tough former sergeant major about forty-three, irreconcilably divorced. One of the youngest was a boy of nineteen who had enlisted in the army, then got right out again for this junket; he was longing for adventures with lots of shooting, perhaps because he was small for his age. A majority came from the South and West, and Texans were the largest group from any state. (p. 60)

More specific are the statements of motivation in individual pilot's memoirs. R.T. Smith begins his *Tale of a Tiger* with the steady half-muffled roar from what he calls "The weary old Wright Cyclone up front" grinding away on a practice flight over a bleakly arid south Texas that "wilted in the heat and humidity of early summer, 1941"—descriptions indicative of "the persistent feeling of boredom and frustration which I felt in my role as flight instructor" (p. 5). Assigned to Randolph Field when his friends were sent off to postings with fighter squadrons, Smith felt trapped by a new regulation which set height limits for such duty: five feet ten inches, well below his towering six feet four. When Skip Adair, the AVG recruiter making rounds of Air Corps bases, passed through San Antonio, Smith and a friend used a bottle of whiskey to help equivocate their way through an interview meant to determine their proficiency in flying the P-40 (they had none whatsoever, never having seen this type of plane). Once accepted, however, they fit in as well as any of the volunteers, some of whom had trained to fly dive bombers or flying boats. Gathering at a San Francisco hotel prior to their Far East departure, the AVG recruits hit it off well. "And for the first time in a long while I felt completely at home," Smith sighs. "These were my kind of guys, all of them, seeking adventure and willing to accept the risks and pay the price" (p. 38). By September 17 he's in the cockpit of a P-40, "grinning and chuckling to myself like a kid with a beautiful new toy, and feeling terribly self-satisfied. Somehow I'd managed to beat the system and the eggheads in the pentagon with their silly rules" (p. 68). By late December, when his old military colleagues are celebrating Christmas on such lonely, boring duty as guarding the Panama Canal, Smith is shooting down Japanese bombers over Rangoon, fighting a war they wouldn't see for almost another year.

Boredom, rather than a shoot-'em-up mentality, is also what brought Charlie Bond into the AVG. Enlisting in the Army as early as 1935 with hopes of becoming a pursuit pilot, he wound up being trained on bombers instead. With nothing to bomb, the Air Corps assigned him to the Air Transport Command, ferrying Lockheed Hudsons from the factory in Burbank, California, to a base in Montreal, Canada, from where the British would accept them as Lend-Lease. The job was "dull" and "routine," as Bond complains at the start of A Flying Tiger's Diary (p. 16). There seems no way out until a friend of a friend (the ubiquitous Skip Adair) makes contact with the AVG pitch. Bond's enthusiasm overshadows his lack of time on fighters. In sorting out his motives, he admits that "the lure of adventure in a foreign country on the other side of the world was exciting," but "more important, however, was the unique and ideal manner in which this opportunity served to satisfy my dreams: a chance to get back into fighters, a chance for combat experience which might help me secure a regular commission, and a chance to earn fast money which would put me in a position to buy my parents a home" (p. 20).

And so there it is, last but important among all the enticements to China, money. More than one Flying Tiger will link such earnings, large as they are, with the desire to buy his folks a home; as often as not, the home is for a widowed mother, replete with gardens for vegetables and flowers, sentiments whose context (letters home on the eve of battle) argues for their sincerity. In one case, money wasn't even the volunteer's idea, but that of his commanders: Pappy Boyington was almost literally drummed out of the Marine Corps until he could catch up on alimony and pay off a host of other debts that had made him a disgrace to his unit. Yet in a few others, economics were more bald faced and mercenary than going after Japanese bombers for pay. Shortly after Paul Frillmann's group of fresh recruits reached Burma, several resigned—a few because the rough conditions weren't what they bargained for, but many as part of a premeditated plan to get out of their military enlistments so that they could accept high-paying jobs with the airlines, eager to hire now that experienced pilots were becoming scarce.

Ironically, it was as a private corporation doing its business in the air that the American Volunteer Group was organized. It would be kept in order not as a military outfit but as an airline, the critical nature of flying being the determinant for order rather than any abstract military code. Charlie Bond, with some of the longest service experience and perhaps the firmest plans for a lifetime Air Force career (he eventually retired as a major general), writes optimistically of this intent in his diary for November 13, 1941, the day after his own group of AVG personnel reached Rangoon:

> The setup is not as bad as some of us were led to believe by rumors from disgruntled ones. The American Volunteer Group is headed by Colonel Claire Chennault with a very small administrative staff of selected men from volunteers from the Navy, Army Air Corps, and Marines. We have about one hundred pilots and about two hundred maintenance and support personnel. No military titles. Everything is run like a

civilian business, somewhat like an American airline company. However, there is an underlying, subconscious aura of military relations between the officers, pilots and staff, and the enlisted men, maintenance and support people. Discipline is more a matter of each individual's own behavior and his personal regard for the other man. (p. 41)

R.T. Smith credits the same ideal as working toward what he calls "a much more democratic atmosphere" in which these freedoms were seldom abused. "Actually," he notes, "I think it tended to keep us on our toes," citing one of his bad landings for which he was comically chewed out by his ground crew. "Imagine something like that happening in the Air Corps or on the deck of a carrier!" he exclaims (p. 71). Olga Greenlaw sums up the motivational inducement by emphasizing the "one vital difference between the AVG and a regular service unit," one that eclipsed any question of discipline: "Our boys were free to resign whenever they wished—which can't be done in the Army, Navy or Marines" (p. 50). Her final proof of their merit is how few of them failed to stick it out.

Like Paul Frillmann, Olga Greenlaw had a chance for special insights into the Flying Tigers. Together with the group's nurses, she was one of just three women working with these three hundred men for a year so far from home. As wife of Claire Chennault's chief assistant, she was privileged to inside information and present when important decisions were made. As group diarist, she kept track of everything official that happened; with several pilots she shared deep emotional attachments, serving as their confidant and learning more about them than their leader ever could. She was happy that Chennault was "by no means a spit-and-polish general" but felt that among all the freedom from restrictions he allowed "that he was too lenient about the use of liquor, particularly with the men [serving as ground crew], and that the Group as a whole would have benefited by a bit more iron-handed discipline" (p. 96). The worst examples of rowdiness, to the point of brutal assaults and other outright criminal activity, happened among what in a military unit would have been the enlisted men; the flyers themselves were former officers in a day when the Air Corps and Navy demanded a minimum of two years of college before being accepted and when college itself was more restrictive. Yet even the flyers could shock an upper-crust blueblood such as Joe Alsop, whose first words for them in his own memoir are that "The pilots were a motley bunch, largely untrained as fighter pilots and hardly disciplined as men" (p. 173). Olga Greenlaw was prone to dismiss their misbehavior as having a few too many drinks at the Burmese railroad station restaurant and shooting up the village "Red Gulch style" (p. 55), a reputation Robert Lee Scott characterizes in *Flying Tiger: Chennault of China* as that of "pirates, or western bad men, and they were just about as hard to handle" (p. 21)—a judgment he later modifies as an act put on to scandalize regular service personnel, including himself (p. 58). Much of the worst behavior was attributable to the ugly American syndrome, as when a crew chief beat up a French doctor who refused to perform an abortion on the chief's Burmese girlfriend. Part of it was the tit-for-tat game played with authority: when Chennault appointed a formal provost marshal, two technicians beat *him* up on principle. But at least a few of the goings on were serious. Innuendoes from other memoirs are given full treatment by Pappy Boyington in his novel *Tonya* (1960), in which Chennault is a wencher, Olga Greenlaw shares his bed and many others', Harvey Greenlaw is a petty martinet, Paul Frillmann is a drunk, and one of the pilots of the AVG's communications flight is a big-time drug runner on the international scene. And before the AVG left Burma there was no small amount of black marketeering, fueled as it was by the abundance of military stores being abandoned in retreat. When Chennault fired the culprits it only gave them more freedom in which to conduct their illicit trade.

"There are many 'red asses' and 'independents' in this outfit," Charlie Bond complains to his diary on January 16, 1942, after almost a full month of hostile operations. "It is pathetic! I get quite frustrated and enraged" (p. 76). These are the words, of course, of a future major general. But even as a flyer disposed toward adventuring with the Flying Tigers he finds his patience tested by lapses in performance that could have been so easily prevented with a minimum of service discipline. Animosities developed between Robert "Sandy" Sandell and the men under his leadership in the 1st AVG Squadron, weakening the unit's effectiveness. In the 2nd Squadron, pilot Raymond Hastey had a rough experience after taking off from the base at Mingaladon to defend Rangoon on January 28, 1942. Not only was his plane hit, but after bailing out he was shot at in his parachute; startled by such realities of war, he refused to fly again, asking for and getting ground duties instead. This was the same day and at the same field where a Japanese pilot deliberately crashed his disabled fighter into a just-landed Tomahawk, sacrificing himself in the samurai tradition of *jibaku*, which in modern times had become part of accepted military practice. As Daniel Ford notes of this occasion, "The contrast with Chennault's free-wheeling mercenaries could not have been greater" (p. 210).

Most examples of less than ship-shape behavior, however, tend to be comic and derive in fact from the AVG's essentially good nature. Their casual, even loose, conduct was characteristic not of malcontents but of people having a good time, of young men supremely enjoying what they are doing. At Kyedaw, the training base borrowed from the RAF, Chennault's flyers found themselves guarded by a platoon of Gurkhas, sturdy little Nepalese troops symbolic of Britain's colonial armies and quite in character by only knowing a few words (for minimal commands) of English. In *Tale of a Tiger*, R.T. Smith enjoys telling how he and his friends would be returning late at night from celebrations in Toungoo and have to answer the Gurkha guard's challenge, "Halt! Who goes there?" To the tough little soldier standing there with rifle at ready, a tipsy Flying Tiger might yell back, "Japanese spy!," a formulation which inevitably prompted the Gurkha to lower his rifle and sing out cheerfully, "Poss, Jopponese spy!" (p. 73). A similar language game was played later on in China, when the operations of Chennault's new regular air force were hampered and harassed by the leader's old nemesis from service days, Colonel Clayton Bissell, serving in India as a temporary brigadier general simply so he could outrank Chennault and keep firm control over his supplies. Frustrations got so bad that the second generation Tigers sought comfort in teaching their Chinese ground crews just a minimal three words of English, a phrase each innocent crewman thought was a pleasant greeting, so pleased did each American visitor seem when pulling up for a refueling and being hailed with a hearty "Piss on Bissell!" When the acting brigadier was eventually received this way himself, the Tigers' hilarity could scarcely be contained.

If these pilots did not take a prissy, regulation-conscious officer like Bissell seriously, neither did they demand heavy formalities for themselves. After all, they were flying worn out, poorly maintained, ill-supplied aircraft in a region with some of the worst flying weather in the world—monsoons in the summer, haze and dust other times, with an inhospitable landscape below should anything go wrong. Even navigation was a joke, as electronic aids were nonexistent and accurate maps unobtainable. They described their flying standards as IFR: not for "Instrument Flight Rules," as might apply were there facilities for using their instruments, but rather "I follow railroads." Good hearted as they were, the AVG met almost everyone with good humor. Consider how on February 4, 1942, Ed Liebolt and Einar Mickelson of the 3rd Squadron welcomed two unexpected visitors to their base at Kunming. As one was a beautiful Chinese woman, Chennault's men were hospitable to the point of putting the make on her. As she responded with courtesy that to a young American might seem flirtatious, they suggested she ditch the older gentleman who seemed to be with her. Only when Chinese servants at the AVG hostel recognized her as Madame Chiang did a shocked Liebolt and Mickelson scramble to retrieve the Generalissimo they'd left stranded on the runway. A month later, as the rest of the AVG left a collapsing Burma for safety in China, Paul Frillmann's contingent met up with the U.S. Army ground commander, "Vinegar Joe" Stilwell, who lived up to his nickname by dressing down the volunteers for their poor image. Frillmann's men were in fact the most presentable contingent thereabouts, as in the middle of Stilwell's diatribe a carload of unsupervised ground crew drove up with a supply of contraband, Anglo-Burmese girlfriends, and bottles of liquor, the last of which they were waving merrily from the window. No account survives of the general's words to *them*.

Boozing with party girls was not an atypical image for flyers, particularly irregular adventurers like the AVG. Homosexual behavior was more unusual, but it too made its contribution to the group's image, eventually in a very big way. Among the troublemakers Chennault weeded out were clerks Ken Sanger and Larry Moore; the colonel's objection was that they were lovers and therefore unsuited for service. Their revenge was to take their firsthand knowledge of the AVG and concoct it into a story saleable to Hollywood. By June 1942, while their former colleagues were still flying and fighting in China, Republic Studios had their movie in production, and even though Chennault's intercession with Republic got the two men removed from active participation in the filming, much damage was done. Starring John Wayne, the film as released drew great attention to the AVG's exploits, but very little of director David Miller's *Flying Tigers* conformed with fact. No pilot in Chennault's squadrons ever caused the death of colleagues by selfishly going after kills for bonuses, and none of them ever practiced their own version of *jibaku* by making his copilot bail out before he sacrificed his own life by diving their aircraft into a Japanese supply train. As an apotheosis of male love and transcendental bonding, the flyers' behavior made for a stirring plot, thoroughly convincing if one ignored the fact that Chennault's American Volunteer Group flew only single-seat fighters.

Other media also did their best to enhance the Flying Tigers legend. As matters of fact, while operating as just one squadron at a time AVG flyers had inflicted such high losses on Japanese bomber groups that Rangoon was held three months longer than anyone might have hoped for, allowing a somewhat more orderly retreat by the British into India and giving Chennault more time to establish operations in his original destination, China. Also established as fact were the extremely long odds at which the Flying Tigers fought; to merely survive, their success ratio would have to be high. As it happened, the inflation of claims inevitable in the confusion of battle produced figures that let American newspaper correspondents have a field day. In *The Flying Tigers*, Russell Whelan describes the formula one reporter used and adds his own exuberance to stir his book's 1942 readership at a point when American successes were still an exception rather than the rule:

Leland Stowe, in Rangoon for the *Chicago Daily News* foreign service, essayed a breakdown of the results attained by the AVG, and reached a total of one hundred and thirty Jap planes as "truly conservative." Of this number, Stowe figured that about forty per cent, or fifty-two planes, were bombers, with crews from five to eight men each. Striking an average of six and one-half men for each Jap bomber, he placed the Japs' personnel losses in bombers at three hundred and thirty-eight men, plus seventy-eight Jap pilots killed in single-seat fighters, or a total of four hundred and sixteen crew losses for the Japanese.

"In these engagements the AVG lost five pilots killed in action and one believed taken prisoner," wrote Stowe. (One of these, Bert Christman, was "murdered" while descending in his parachute.) "That number of six Americans lost can be placed alongside of more than four hundred Jap airmen who have been wiped out by American fighter pilots in the Burma war theater.

"All feelings of national pride can be put aside in reporting this outstanding and historical achievement of the AVG in Burma during the last seven weeks. It is an achievement which certainly has very rarely been equalled anywhere since the war began, and possibly not equalled by the same number of airmen operating with ground crews which are very far below the regulation size used by the U.S. Army Air Forces.

"Nevertheless, despite the Nazis' flair for making exorbitant claims for their pilots, even the Germans have never claimed that their squadrons have eliminated enemy air personnel at anything remotely approaching a ratio of six pilots lost against four hundred or more in enemy flying personnel.

"Fortune gave the AVG an opportunity to turn the air war's tide over Burma, but to these young Americans belongs credit for having risen magnificently to an opportunity in which odds seemed seriously against them."

In that dispatch Leland Stowe was straining for conservativism
with both fists. Four hundred-odd against six! Shades of Frank
Merriwell, Tom Swift, Tarzan, and Superman! There had never
been anything like this since Cain tackled Abel in the first
recorded battle of history. (pp. 120-22)

Other reporters used such images as the Spartans at
Thermopylae or a few rowboats engaging the Spanish Ar-
mada. In these cases imagery told a more accurate story, for
Chennault's men were indeed grossly outnumbered. But nowhere near 130 Japanese planes were shot down, and no Japanese bomber carried a crew of eight. Even the lurid reference
to Christman's death ignored the fact that international law
and the covenants of war allowed for the shooting of enemy
airmen in parachutes if they were descending over their own
territory, from which they could presumably return to combat. As for numbers, the validity of their rhetoric is confirmed
by Olga Greenlaw, who for her own readers in a 1943 still
suggestive as being a long way from victory was able to put it
bluntly and accurately:

> The situation looked gloomy indeed when all of a sudden
> out of nowhere came a blazing flash of light. A handful of
> unknown American youngsters in airplanes which had been
> much maligned by the British and Americans, completely on
> their own and constantly heckled by a hundred official,
> political and international stupidities, slashed through the blue
> Burmese skies and not only kicked the daylights out of all the
> Japs in sight but proved, mathematically, that one good
> American is a match for any twenty Japanese—and thereby
> saved the white man's ego from a total breakdown. (p. 49)

Whatever the imagery, there was more than enough real
success in the Flying Tigers' exploits for them to become
genuine heroes. Hometowns across America that previously
could look only to casualty lists from Pearl Harbor for a local connection to the war now had boys in the AVG to be
proud of. When Ken Jernstedt of Yamhill, Oregon, took part
in a successful attack against the Moulmein airfield now in
Japanese hands, no less a figure than the governor of Oregon responded with an internationally transmitted radio
message, asking the young man what type of airplane his

fellow citizens should buy and send over to his squadron in Burma. Like the Spitfire Funds that rallied patriotic support in Britain, this gesture would let Americans feel they were participating. That the contribution was to a winning effort was clarified by no less a personage than Winston Churchill, who in February 1942 described the AVG's efforts in defense of Rangoon as comparable in character to the RAF's efforts in the Battle of Britain. From this man, whose noblest oratory had been inspired by the heroism of that particular fight, no higher commendation was possible.

Almost half a century later, and writing from the responsible position of a retired Air Force major general, Charlie Bond could look back on this first success. Postwar documentation let him get the numbers right; even in their lesser scale they still seemed overwhelming, for by any measure they most certainly were. More important, the perspective he took then and takes again now, as he prepares *A Flying Tiger's Diary* for publication, clarifies the AVG's importance:

> The first taste of battle—just three engagements over China and Burma—demonstrated our ability and training as fighter pilots. During that first week of action the AVG destroyed fifty-five enemy bombers and fighters while losing only five Tomahawks. Unfortunately, two of our colleagues were killed, but at the same time two hundred enemy airmen were either killed or captured.
>
> We were shattering the myth that the Japanese Air Force was invincible. (p. 78)

At Odds in China

– • – From the ground in Burma, matters looked less sanguine than they seemed in the air. When the 3rd Squadron of the AVG was relieved from its initial defense of Rangoon, one of its ground crewmen confessed his terror to radioman Robert M. Smith.

"It was horrible, Smitty, it was horrible," the man reports in Smith's *With Chennault in China*. "Sixty-five tons of bombs were dropped on Rangoon. It was worse than anything the British saw at London. I never want to see another like it" (p. 46). Everything the squadron crew had on the ground was flattened; safety could be found only deep in a slit trench. One of the volunteers never made it out of the operations office, which took a direct hit: "I saw parts of him hanging from a barbed wire fence. Oh, it was horrible, Smitty, horrible. I never want to see it again" (p. 49).

But it did happen again, and again several times over, between late December 1941 and early March when the city eventually fell. With the first raids Chinese coolies abandoned the docks and large numbers of Indian office workers and shopkeepers packed up and headed home. "That is a sight," Smith's friend marvels, "Rangoon walking back to India" (p. 49). Chaplain Paul Frillmann complains of an even more pervasive weakness, extending to the British who he felt no longer had the heart to care for their colonial system. "Inside Rangoon," he notes in *China: The Remembered Life*, "it was appallingly clear that this capital and single metropolis of Burma was crumbling in defeat before a single Japanese foot soldier had crossed the border" (p. 105). When time for evacuation came, civil order had almost totally broken down. "Most of the whites were gone," Olga Greenlaw recalls in *The Lady and the Tigers*. "The lepers and the insane had been turned loose. Rioting, thieving and looting were going on. The police had lost control over the natives. No one was safe in the streets at night" (p. 101).

Colonel Chennault's volunteers were part of this exodus. With an avalanche of supplies abandoned on the docks, they grabbed what they could, later uncrating their loot to discover, according to Duane Schultz in *The Maverick War*, "a five-year supply of shoelaces, a year's worth of facial tissues, and a small mountain of kitchen cleanser" (p. 209). But no toothpaste—for brushing their teeth the men would have to use something from another case, a hoard of Bristol cream sherry. To reach their new base in Kunming, China, ground elements of the AVG would have to negotiate the tricky Burma Road, the route they had come to defend and over which more serious supplies were supposed to have made their way to Chiang Kai-shek's beleaguered people.

Along with the losses of Hong Kong and especially Singapore, the fall of Burma put Britain in a dangerous position. Were Japan now to take the next step and capture India, an assault could be made onward to the Middle East, attacking Britain's desert army from the rear and securing the Mediterranean for the Axis. If China, too, were removed from the conflict, Japanese resources could be directed more powerfully toward maintaining early gains in the Pacific. Allied strategy recognized both elements in reorganizing for a China-Burma-India theater; the middle factor had been lost, but if each end was secure a more reasonable situation in the Far East might be obtained. In the Royal Air Force, squadrons that had been wiped out in Singapore and Rangoon were reformed, albeit with more obsolescent equipment:

Mohawk and early marque Hurricane fighters flew through-out 1942 until Spitfires replaced them in 1943, while Blenheims did the heavier work until modern Beaufighters and a few Mosquitoes arrived. In China the American Volunteer Group continued in its efforts to prevent a Japanese free hand, only near the end obtaining a few Curtiss P-40E Kittyhawks, a plane better equipped for the unit's enhanced duties in ground attack. Still, the core of Chennault's outfit was what remained of his original one hundred P-40C Toma-hawks and pilots to fly them.

Away from the rat race of Burma and reestablished in their intended role, the AVG became even more aware of the long odds at which it fought and difficult conditions in which it had to operate. Small as it was, the original number of one hundred planes and pilots had suffered from hid-eous attrition even before the first enemy bullet was fired or bomb was dropped. Of his one hundred pilot recruits, only ninety-nine embarked from the United States. The man Chennault wanted most was not among them, his attempt to get a passport foiled by the State Department's worry over the very talents his new boss wanted to employ—for Albert "Ajax" Baumler had already flown as a mercenary for the Loyalists during the Spanish Civil War, shooting down eight German and Italian planes in 1938. There were only ninety-nine P-40s as well, for one was inadvertently dropped into Rangoon harbor during the unloading process. The ranks of both men and planes thinned rapidly, thanks to resignations either planned from the start (using military releases for AVG service to get freed for lucrative airline employment) or be-cause of dismay at local conditions; P-40s were lost in flying accidents and severely damaged during training mishaps on the ground. By the time the volunteer group disbanded, on July 4, 1942, Chennault had been forced to discharge ad-ditional men for disciplinary reasons. All told, twenty-two pilots and forty-three ground crew did not serve out their contracts, a failure rate of almost twenty-five percent.

A large part of the problem with both men and planes was the way the AVG had to be trained. Time limits made for severe pressures both on the American Volunteer Group and the USAAF's 23rd Fighter Group that beginning in the summer of 1942 replaced them. The latter was the first U.S. combat group to be formed in a combat zone during World War II. Such formation even in peacetime is a major organizational job. As Carl Molesworth notes in *Sharks over China*, "It was standard practice for USAAF fighter groups to form in the United States and train for six months or more before they ever reached foreign soil, much less encountered an enemy aircraft" (p. 5). Chennault did it in combat areas twice, with minimal breathing space for the AVG in Burma and none whatsoever for the 23rd Fighter Group in China.

At least his Army Air Force pilots in the 23rd had taken their Primary and Basic Training according to the same method and in Advanced were given extensive experience in fighters. Less than a fifth of the AVG was so qualified. Many were Navy or Marine flyers, whose expertise with single-engine planes was directed to operating them from carrier decks. Others were trained as dive bombers, while a few had flown mostly multiengine bombers, transports, or—most preposterously, considering what Chennault would be asking of them from day one—flying boats. Aircraft losses due to accidents outstripped what would be a normal group's anticipated attrition from combat. Less than two months before his flyers would be facing hundreds of Japanese aggressors, Chennault's men were piling up their P-40s in alarming numbers. Such doings prompted one calendar date, November 3, 1941, to be long remembered as "Circus Day," on which during the hours of daylight one Tomahawk leveled off too early, dropping so hard it burst a tire and veered from the runway (a flaw typical of flying boat pilots, by habit thinking of their cockpits as being much higher up), another angled off into the trees where its landing gear collapsed, a third ground-looped on landing, damaging its wheels, while at dispersal a pair of P-40s chewed off the tails of two others while a third plane braked too hard and nosed up. The day's net loss was eight planes, a greater number than the Japanese would take down in any single action.

The particular batch of P-40s purchased for the AVG

made for further hardships. At the Curtiss-Wright factory in Buffalo, New York, they had been manufactured for Britain and hence came off the line with RAF specifications. That meant wing guns that took .303-caliber ammunition, instead of .50 caliber like American fighters of the time. There were no .303-caliber bullets in China, however, and getting them supplied from abroad was a continuing problem. Because the RAF used a different type of radio and would be doing installations themselves, these Tomahawks left the factory with none whatsoever. Chennault had hoped to get what the Army Air Force was using, but those were denied to Chiang's buyers; all they could purchase were "Piper Cub sportplane radio sets," as radioman Robert M. Smith describes in *With Chennault in China*, "providing us with another hazard in our operations because these could not stand up in continual combat and often failed at embarrassing times" (p. 11). There were no bomb racks or drop tanks either, and so these had to be improvised. Worst of all, the three squadrons of Tomahawks were delivered with no spare parts whatsoever, not even a spark plug. As replacements were needed, they had to be scrounged from all over Southeast Asia. This was one of Joe Alsop's jobs, seeking help from MacArthur in Manila and from the British in Singapore and Karachi. He was returning through Hong Kong when that city fell to the Japanese, putting him in alien internment for several months before he could use his old connections in journalism to talk his way out, eventually making his way back to Chennault's staff.

Compounding the problem of flying American planes built to British specifications in the nether reaches of a China almost completely cut off from supplies was the fact that the purchase and maintenance of these planes was from start to finish a commercial, rather than a military, agreement. As a neutral when the AVG was organized, the United States could not sell military equipment to a belligerent air force. Put bluntly, there had to be a cover organization with whom to do the dealing, and thus CAMCO, the Central Aircraft Manufacturing Corporation, was formed by H.H. Kung, one of Madame Chiang's brothers-in-law, and the American

William Pawley, a businessman with interests in Chinese aviation. Chennault had known Pawley since 1935, meeting him at the Miami Air Races where the Air Corps' aerobatics act made its first contact with recruiters for the Chinese Air Force, the seed that later brought Chennault to China.

From the very start of AVG planning Pawley made trouble. Because another hat he wore was that of agent for Curtiss-Wright sales in China, he demanded his customary ten percent commission, even though he had nothing to do with agenting the deal and was himself, in legal terms, the purchaser. This wrangling set schedules back several months, forcing the AVG to train in Burma rather than China and throwing it almost at once into the battle for Rangoon. Once the AVG was established, dealings with Pawley only got worse. With the planes taking a terrible beating during training and by December suffering combat damage as well, CAMCO reneged on its agreement to repair P-40s at its base in Loiwing, where Pawley was making better money assembling trainers and CW-21 Demon fighters he'd sold directly to China. A vicious war of words erupted between the two men, each feeling his reputation was being damaged by repercussions reaching to Chiang and Roosevelt.

Because of his success with the AVG and heroic leadership of the air war in China all the way to the summer of 1945, Claire Chennault had the last word against Bill Pawley. *Way of a Fighter* is not a mean-spirited autobiography; Generals Bissell and Stilwell, who caused the Flying Tigers much trouble and often for relatively petty motives, are handled with surprising equanimity and understanding. But for the general partner of CAMCO Chennault has no good words at all:

> I have always suspected that Pawley, like the Japanese, thoroughly believed the British and American intelligence reports that the AVG would not last three weeks in combat. At any rate on the occasions when he had a chance to provide the AVG with badly needed assistance, Pawley exhibited what I considered a remarkable lack of co-operation. It was only after the AVG's combat record had made the organization world famous that Pawley made strenuous efforts to have himself

identified with it, even to the extent of attempting to secure an honorary membership of the Flying Tigers Incorporated, the only authentic postwar organization of former AVG men, by offering a ten-thousand-dollar contribution to the corporation's funds. His offer was flatly rejected by the membership, who apparently felt that a few repaired P-40's during the dark days of 1941-42 would have been more valuable to them than a postwar check. After a succession of wartime manufacturing ventures, Pawley embarked on a diplomatic career as ambassador to Peru and Brazil. No doubt he found the Medal for Merit awarded him for "organizing the Flying Tigers" useful to his new work. (pp. 132-33)

In early 1942, with Pawley off to a new venture in India, Chennault turned to the Generalissimo for help. Chiang arranged for the Chinese manager of CAMCO to continue repairing AVG planes while plans were made to have the Chinese government buy out Pawley's interest in the corporation. This militarized the operation, but that was no longer a problem because the United States had entered the war as China's ally.

Having fought a withdrawing action from Rangoon northward toward the border, the AVG spent its last three months operating more systematically against the Japanese. Their first operation, on December 20, 1941, had defended Kunming from Japanese bombers who heretofore had enjoyed free reign over the city. Now that the defense of Rangoon was over, Chennault's pilots could use China as a base from which to take the war back to the Japanese. Supply lines via road and rail were interdicted; Burmese bases that had once been the RAF's and AVG's own were attacked as enemy forces used them as staging areas for their advance toward India. Thailand and French Indo-China, occupied by the Japanese early on, now became Flying Tiger targets. Chinese bombers were being escorted as far as Hanoi and Haiphong. Kill ratios remained high, but the stress of operations, especially under adverse conditions, took its toll on morale. The fact that the United States was now in the war did not help; at best, the AVG could pride themselves that they had been ahead of the time in their sentiments and were now vindicated, but the more predominant attitude was one of feeling abandoned, because so far American might had supplied them with next to nothing and sent in no pilot reinforcements at all. By spring of 1942, only about half of their original ninety-nine Tomahawks were still flyable, and most were in miserable shape; not a single one would have been let off the ground, much less sent into combat, had this been a regular outfit operating in the USAAF. When on April 15, 1942, Colonel Chennault of the Chinese Air Force was taken back into the American military as a colonel in the Army Air Force and almost immediately promoted to brigadier general, some pilots were resentful. As far as his relations with the AVG, a general's stars meant nothing positive. His flyers were still civilians, not subject to military orders; persuasion and the discipline of a well-run business remained the only ways to get things done. Negatively, their leader's new status made some men feel the Army was taking over with no benefits to themselves. Aggressive, ill-tempered, and loutish behavior, such as had been restricted before to ground crews and technicians, broke out in several instances among the pilots. Six of them quit, including Pappy Boyington on April 20; though later hailed as a hero both for his Flying Tiger and subsequent Black Sheep Squadron service with the Marines, he was written off the AVG books by Chennault with a dishonorable discharge, for the record considered a deserter.

Strains and stresses had been obvious for some time, starting with Charlie Bond's diary notations and surfacing through various attempts to revise the command structure. Oddly enough, Boyington emerged as Bond's partner in trying to maintain tighter order, at least during duty hours. Bond himself worried whether the AVG could survive a concentrated Japanese attack and became well enough known for his views that other concerned flyers flocked to him, while Dr. Lewis Richard and chaplain Paul Frillmann sought him out for late-night sessions devoted to seeking the larger good. As early as January 2, 1942, one finds Bond confiding to his *Flying Tiger's Diary* that "I went to bed wondering if I were now becoming another 'chaplain' along with the Padre" (p. 70).

Provocation for a more serious type of revolt arrived on

April 9 in the person of Chiang Kai-shek. The Generalissimo was visiting Kunming with some bad news and an even less heartening request. His Chinese ground forces were being beaten back through Burma. Already pushed past the former AVG training base at Kyedaw Field near Toungoo, these troops would have to rally or everything would collapse to the north, putting the enemy on Chiang's doorstep. British forces, more concerned with preventing a quick Japanese thrust toward India, felt the Chinese were not doing enough to stem the larger tide. Therefore Chiang reversed roles with Chennault and sought to give his chief air advisor advice on how to best use the AVG. Could not low-level flights be made above the front lines to inspire the Chinese troops? There was not much enemy air action at this juncture, but as "morale missions" the sight of P-40s sporting the Chinese National star could make a real difference to how the ground fighting went.

As events transpired, the low-level morale missions led to the greatest internal crisis in AVG history. In a footnote to his own first diary entry about these missions in *Tale of a Tiger,* R.T. Smith lays out the essentials from the pilots' point of view: "Toungoo was more than 300 miles from Loiwing, which meant having to stop and refuel enroute, then fly into enemy territory at low altitude with several Jap fighter bases nearby. Perhaps it's understandable that we were not terribly enthusiastic about this idea" (p. 260). Navigation was never easy in Burma, and the end-of-winter stubble-burning practiced by the local rice farmers produced a haze that made any operations below customary safe altitude a nuisance to fly and a dangerous risk. In a contemporary entry Smith writes that "Chennault wants the Toungoo job done still, but we're all agin' it. Think we'll go down + strafe Jap fields instead" (p. 263). It was this style of freelancing insubordination that prompted Chiang's visit to AVG Headquarters up in Kunming, urging that the Loiwing squadron get serious about orders. As a result, nine planes from the 2nd Squadron (seven of them new P-40E Kittyhawks) came down to fly three-plane patrols to Toungoo three times a day, racking up numbers meant to impress the Generalissimo. "It's a foolish mission with lots of risks," Smith complains again, "+ not much chance to do any good" (p. 273). Yet it had to be flown, for Chennault himself accompanied the fighters in a CNAC transport and settled down to stay a while.

Within a week, Chennault was a very angry man, which was understandable, for no sooner had he arrived to ride herd on the independents at Loiwing than other pilots started filling out their resignations back at Kunming. With pressure mounting on both sides, something had to snap, and it did on Saturday, April 18. Some Tomahawks, which by tacit agreement between Chennault and his pilots were reserved for local defense, were ordered to join the better-equipped Kittyhawks to escort six RAF Blenheims on a low-level raid against the Cheng Mai airfield deep in enemy territory. Unexpected Japanese fighters had made a shambles of the morale missions, as the P-40s were drawn up too high to be seen by the Chinese troops yet still positioned with inferior altitude. Now a low-level escort mission would expose Chennault's pilots to antiaircraft fire as well. Luckily the mission was scrubbed when the Blenheims were delayed. But inspirational flying over the front lines was to continue— "Our twelve ships against the whole damn Jap Air Force," as R.T. Smith put it. "It seems mighty futile to all of us," he continues, "+ we're wondering what's taking the United States so long to get something over here. At this rate, our morale won't be very good fast. Phooey!" (p. 282).

"Off duty today," Smith notes for the day following, April 18, "+ all hell broke loose." There had been a Japanese observation plane over the field to shoot down, but the real fireworks came that evening when Chennault, still ostensibly a colonel in the Chinese Air Force and exercising only civilian control over his contract employees, called a meeting with his AVG flyers who were more and more acting like men soon to be out of control:

> It was to tell us that we were expected to go on any missions
> assigned or else resign. Some of these missions planned we
> consider pretty bad—suicide in fact. Col. Chennault said he
> was now a Brig. Gen., U.S. Army taking orders from Gen.

Stilwell. We all got a load off our chest as to how we felt.—
About not getting any reinforcements + being expected to fight
the whole Jap Air Force etc. So, all pilots here got together, had
a meeting, + voted to resign in protest. Twenty-eight of us out
of 34 signed the sheet, + it is to be given to the Col. tomorrow.
 So, either we'll get some concessions or be going home soon.
We all want to stay + fight back, but we can't go on an offensive with twelve airplanes, especially ones in their condition.
Motor failures are becoming frequent, plenty other troubles.

Charlie Bond, whose insight into what became generally accepted as "the pilots' mutiny" would have been especially valuable, given his fear that something of this order
was coming, was a continent and a half away at this time, in
Karachi to help ferry back a flight of new P-40E Kittyhawks.
Paul Frillmann had been in Loiwing for a few days just before and could see how desperate the men had become; yet
by April 18 he had returned to headquarters at Kunming
and other than understanding how the showdown seemed
inevitable his own *China: The Remembered Life* can offer no
firsthand account of the confrontation. Olga Greenlaw, however, reports uniquely on its immediate aftermath, indicating exactly what set the pilots off. She and her husband had
been coming up the Burma Road with the last AVG forces
withdrawing to China. The Greenlaws met up with Chennault at Loiwing, near the Burmese border, where they resumed their staff duties and picked up on all the doings of
the days before.

 First to interest Olga was news of Pappy Boyington's
resignation. There is ample evidence in both her memoirs
and Boyington's novel that the two were lovers—one of several such relationships maintained by this exotically beautiful wife of a much older and laughably remote husband.
One of Chennault's most trusted squadron leaders, David
Lee "Tex" Hill, told her how it happened. "He got into trouble
with Bob Neale," another pilot to whom Chennault had del-
egated authority; "—reported drunk at night alert. Greg is
easy going, but something happened to him that night."
Accused of drinking on duty, Pappy had taken offense and
resigned on the spot, claiming, "Guess that's what you all

want" (p. 148). This wasn't surprising to Olga, as her lover had confided these sentiments not long before. But Tex Hill's next story was flabbergasting to someone who'd been away and not seen the more recent tensions building:

> "We had a little insurrection here, did you know?"
> I told him I didn't know anything.
> "The Old Man planned a mission escorting some RAF Blenheims. The fellows refused to go, saying it was a suicide mission because the Blenheims are too slow and undependable. We have thirty-two pilots here, and only five of us volunteered to go. Twenty-seven submitted their resignations on one piece of paper."
> "Come outside," I said. "I want to hear the whole story."
> (p. 249)

And so what has begun as a murmured conversation in the squadron mess hall, where the film *Border Town* has been showing, turns into a major piece of exposition reported by one of Chennault's chief loyalists but augmented by one of the renegades as well.

Outside the hall, Greenlaw and Hill bump into R.T. Smith, one of the signers who can explain precisely why Hill and each of his cohorts stayed clear of the revolt. "Tex, you wouldn't refuse the mission because you are a new Squadron Leader, and you thought you might lose your squadron," Smith observes. "Ed Rector," Hill's close friend, "naturally followed your lead." As for Tom Jones and Frank Schiel, the former was returning from an injury and eager for action, while the latter felt obliged "being Intelligence Officer" (p. 249).

Smith continues with his own side of the story: how being made to strafe the Japanese airfield after the Blenheims had bombed would have meant flying into a stirred-up hornets' nest, all surprise having been sacrificed for nothing, because the Blenheims were notoriously inaccurate. As they had before, Smith's cohorts preferred to formulate their own mission plans, in this case hitting the field before dawn. This was less a refusal to obey orders than a case of experience and initiative coming up with a better way to do the job. But as Smith tells Greenlaw, Chennault opened his meeting by laying down the gauntlet in terms that shocked them much more than the original orders:

> "The Colonel said: 'If you want to show the white feather, you can all quit!'
>
> "My God: the white feather!" continued Smith, after what guys like Tex Hill, Lawlor, Keaton, Older and even I have shown we can do in the air, with all the odds against us. I came right out and said he knew damn well we were no cowards. The Colonel said: 'By white feather I mean insubordination.' I insisted it meant 'cowardice.'
>
> "The whole trouble in a nutshell was that we didn't want to escort the Blenheims—not at the time they would be ready. We wanted to get off long before dawn and surprise the Japs. The Blenheims wanted to start at seven! They're late risers."
> (p. 250)

To an American public eager for reports about the fabled and colorful Flying Tigers, news of the mutiny could not be kept secret. Almost coincidental with the 1943 publication of Olga Greenlaw's memoir came *With General Chennault: The Story of the Flying Tigers* (1943), the first inside account of the AVG operation. The author was Robert B. Hotz, assisted by three pilots who had been central to the group's action: George L. "Pappy" Paxton, Robert H. Neale, and Parker S. Dupouy. As the title indicates, Hotz's story portrayed Chennault not just as central character but as the locus of its point of view; the author's own loyalty extended to serving with Chennault's staff for the balance of the war and editing his leader's memoirs for publication in 1949. Hotz handles the situation by citing Pappy Paxton's diary: "The pilots are bitter. They feel Chennault is bloodthirsty and will sacrifice the AVG to the last man. The situation is so hopeless. The demands made on him and the AVG [by the Chinese and British commanders] are so great as to be absolutely impossible, except that Chennault will never admit impossibility. They are expecting us to fight the whole war out here. Chennault is desperate. He keeps telling us the most important thing is to beat the Japs. That is more important than any of us personally, including himself" (p. 216).

By balancing all the accounts and being aware of Chennault's emerging role in the USAAF eventual takeover, it is possible to interpret Paxton's last analysis in broader perspective. Chennault had not been taken back into the Army Air Force, especially at the rank of brigadier general, because of anything he'd done on his own. His claim to fame was the American Volunteer Group and its unique success in an impossibly difficult theater. Were he to lead the subsequent air effort by regular U.S. forces, it would be because he brought the AVG's experience with him as a core of the strategy and hopefully as the backbone of these new forces as well. Without his pilots, mutinous as they were, he was nothing.

Of course the pilots didn't consider their act a mutiny; instead, in the labor-management schematics that were in fact more appropriate to their contractual situation, they considered themselves on strike. Perhaps a wildcat strike, and certainly as an action meant to win concessions rather than end a working relationship, but a labor action nonetheless—which allowed their boss to play his trump card.

"You men realize that this action while facing the enemy can be considered desertion," Hotz quoted by him as saying in a second meeting, one called to answer the pilots' mass resignation. "Under the Articles of War, the punishment for desertion in the face of the enemy is death. Think it over" (p. 216).

If the "white feather" implication of cowardice had been a volatile suggestion, this second charge was inflammatory. But no further outburst came from the disgruntled pilots. Perhaps they had taken to heart Tex Hill's exhortation that although they had come to China as mercenaries, they were now citizens of a country at war with the same foe; at least some thought to duty must now be a consideration. Perhaps it was Hill's rhetoric that prompted Chennault to change the terms from cowardice in the face of danger to desertion under fire. Whatever the motivations of Chennault and his men, the confrontation passed into history with no further reference to their troubles. The resignations were forgotten, and there were no more plans for either Chinese morale missions or low-level RAF escorts.

In postwar years, when the participants had become icons not just of air war history but of American popular culture, accounts of the pilots' revolt outdo each other with open mindedness and generosity. In *Tonya*, Pappy Boyington sets the stage for Tex Hill's speech by making the AVG not just originally mercenary but chasing the dollar as a motive for refusing the escort mission. It was, after all, a ground target in Thailand. "Our contracts state we'll only be called upon to shoot down planes," one of his fictive flyers protests, "and that we'll only get paid for ones the Chinese confirm." It is this objection that prompts an even more noble statement from the Tex Hill stand-in, to the effect that "Maybe I can answer this. Things are different now our country's at war. We're going to have to make sacrifices which weren't originally in the plan" (p. 244). Even the supposedly factual *Baa Baa Black Sheep* embroiders the situation, having Pappy volunteer for the escort mission because extra pay has been offered (p. 94). And so from the pilots' point of view as taken by Boyington, neither the renegades nor the loyalists look good. For his part, Chennault dismisses the incident in just a page and a half of his lengthy *Way of a Fighter*, taking no time for self-justification and admitting that "Personally I agreed with the pilots' views. The missions were unnecessarily dangerous and, with the exception of strafing enemy airdromes, offered no compensating results" (p. 156). But orders were orders, especially when they came to him from the respective Chinese and Anglo-American commanders. With a general's stars on his shoulders, Chennault was presumably becoming a good soldier.

And so with less than two and a half months remaining on their contracts, the men of the AVG got back to fighting their own style of war. Tired and dispirited, with equipment worn out past all hope of even minimally dependable service and facing a strategic situation years away from any hope of major Allied success, they were still able to make a difference in the closer tactical picture. A bridge crossing in the Salween Gorge was crucial to the Japanese advance against retreating Chinese forces, and in May improvised bombing attacks by AVG Kittyhawks blocked the enemy's progress. At a time when China's collapse seemed a possibility, time was bought for more orderly regrouping. By May 1942, the RAF was also reforming squadrons in India to take the air offensive back to Burma. With the Burma Road long gone, air supply over the Himalayas—"the Hump"—was devised as an originally outlandish but ultimately expedient way of keeping China supplied and therefore in the war.

This, however, was the larger strategic picture, and neither Chennault or his men often thought in such terms. Their leader was devoted to perfecting tactics against a well-studied enemy, and the pilots themselves had enough trouble even personalizing their foes. Having left the States in the summer of 1941, a world away from what would become the very different post–Pearl Harbor era, these peacetime careerists had little clear notion of who their enemy was. When combat did ensue, momentarily over Kunming and then most dramatically in the skies above Rangoon at the end of 1941, they could not picture their adversaries as clearly as did the RAF flyers in England, who had seen newsreels of their future foes in action during the Spanish Civil War. The RAF had been on guard against them since the Munich crisis of 1938 and shuddered with the rest of the world at the lightning efficiency of the aerial bombardment of Warsaw. They had been chased off the Continent in the Battle of France, and finally won a stand-off, the Luftwaffe's first, with the Battle of Britain. That last conflict had many qualities of a face-to-face engagement, one in which sportsmanship and occasional acts of chivalry played their part. High-ranking officers from the rival air forces had met at air shows during the 1930s; younger men flying the British and German planes may have vacationed from school terms near each other's home towns. When both took off for action, their own homes lay beneath them. And their front line of action, the English Channel, was the strategic determinant for taking direction toward the war's end, whichever direction that might be.

No such conditions existed in the skies where the American Volunteer Group and Japanese air forces met. Both were flying from strange lands, the Japanese from captured bases in Thailand and Indo-China, the Americans from borrowed fields in a China and Burma they may have never thought about until half a year before. Strangest of all, they were two groups that up to this time had experienced relatively little cultural contact. If there ever were a situation for realizing the militarist's dream of fighting an impersonal, faceless, dehumanized enemy, the air war developing here in 1941 provided it.

R.T. Smith's memories of his first kill are vivid, albeit in a particular way. The occasion was on December 23, 1941, in defense of Rangoon. The contemporaneous notation is adequately descriptive of the event: "Found a bomber away from the formation, made about 3 passes, and on the last one went in to about 50 yds., firing all 6 guns, and he blew up right in front of me + down in flames" (p. 159). The "he" concerned is not a human being in this language but rather the two-engined airplane. Reliving the experience for his diary's amplification and publication in1986, Smith clarifies this intent:

> I learned after only a few passes at the enemy bombers that deflection shooting was for the experts; I was sure I was scoring some hits, but the results were not at all satisfactory. And so I picked out this one bomber, got directly behind him and just under his prop-wash, and opened fire at about 200 yards. I could see my tracers converging on the fuselage and wing roots as I rapidly undertook him but kept firing until he blew up right in my face. His gas tanks exploded in a huge ball of flame, the concussion tossing my plane upward like a leaf. I fought for control, flying through the debris, felt a thud as something hit my left wing, let out a shout of triumph into my oxygen mask and thought By God, I got one of the bastards no matter what happens from now on! I was thinking strictly in terms of "one" plane, not the six or seven faceless individuals, seen only as shadow-figures if at all. (p. 160)

The analysis is technical, the reaction almost scientific in terms of the physical properties of what happens. As the memoirist says, "the bastard" he gets is singular, the plane; the score is now 1-0, not 6 or 7-0 as would be counted in human terms. He does not even pause to consider that the "something" thudding against his wing is the body of a human being, the torso of which would have stayed intact as everything else blew to pieces. As such, the anonymity of Smith's protestation of hatred recorded the day after Pearl Harbor, in which he relishes engagement conditions "made to order for those little yellow Japs" (p. 145), becomes a characterization of the enemy that fails to survive even the first minute of combat.

As part of the first effort to defend Rangoon, Charlie Bond reacts the same way. His diary entry for December 20 records his own actions and those he can see of the enemy: P-40 sight and gun switches flipped on, rear-gun emplacements on the bombers lowered into fighting position. "I was tense but more excited," Bond recognizes. "I was about to taste combat." Yet the motive is impersonal: "I thought in terms of shooting down airplanes and gave no thought to the fact that there were men in those ships" (p. 61). The abstraction of the enterprise shouldn't be cause for dismay. American military flyers were trained to shoot down enemy aircraft, not enemy personnel; far from being hand-to-hand combat, one extremely powerful and complex machine is being engaged against another. Memoirs from the air war in Europe are characterized by similar attitudes, to the point that the writer sometimes expresses surprise to see a person emerging from the plane being shot at. But at that point in narratives from RAF, Luftwaffe, and United States Army Air Force pilots flying in the European theater, human qualities almost at once make a welcomed entrance. Little of that if any happens in stories from the Far East.

Instead, when he could be seen, the enemy was immediately dehumanized. Charlie Bond himself makes the distinction in a diary entry for February 21, 1942, after a ground attack mission. Such engagements were an anomaly for fighter pilots, for in such cases they were able to see the individuality of their enemy and take close account of the damage they were inflicting. They could see men die, men they themselves were killing—just as thoroughly but immensely more observable than an adversary in the air. Yet if Bond could be abstract about his enemies in airplanes, he was much more blunt about victims on the ground, as his diary records:

> I had really been in combat—a lot of it, all kinds, and all day. I had seen war at its worst. That Jap column had been wrecked by .50-caliber slugs tearing the trucks to bits. I saw one Japanese on his horse ducking for cover and I had grinned as I passed over to get a bead on a truck down the line. I'm sure I would have gunned him down just like a truck had I been in the right position. What a business. Like beasts. No thought for life whatsoever. Instead, a feeling of hatred for the Japanese that becomes deeper day by day. (p. 106)

Here the contrasts with memoirs from the European theater are pronounced. Extremely few British or American pilots attacking ground targets on the continent enjoyed seeing their human targets; most abhorred it. Testing their skills against a similarly equipped enemy in the skies was more of a fair fight, and the kill was envisioned as against the machine, not the man in it. In this passage Bond reverses such conventional sentiments by grinning at the sight of a potential victim and admitting that he'd just as soon destroy the individual as the machine. True, after four months overseas in the worst possible conditions he hates the Japanese. From his point of view, they might as well be beasts. But the person with "no thought for life whatsoever" is Charlie Bond, who thereby admittedly lowers himself as well from human status.

In the air, at least, pilots can hope to remove themselves from such sentiments. Bond makes the distinction three weeks earlier, when he taxis past the remains of a Japanese fighter destroyed by its pilot's suicidal crash into a parked Blenheim. "An RAF airman held up a leather helmet with the pilot's head still in it and with parts of his throat hanging down in a bloody mess. With his other hand the airman pointed two fingers skyward in the usual V-for-victory sign. I returned the V-sign and taxied on. I could not, however, return his broad grin" (p. 88).

A grin for the Japanese cavalryman he'd shoot just as soon as the enemy truck, but no grin for the airman with his grisly trophy—from these two passages the value system is clear. Bond has seen himself in bestial terms and deplored it, flying away from an occasion best left on the ground. In this other incident, however, he can maintain a superior position. The ghastly business is done not by him but by an airman, not a flyer but a creature of the ground. The man is not an AVG comrade but someone from a different force, the RAF, where his actions speak of the English lower classes rather than the service's well-bred officer pilots: from a proletarian British perspective, two fingers raised means first of all "up yours," a crudity being conveyed to the deceased Japanese. Bond, however, chooses to take it in the finer sense of Churchill's famous double entendre. Most emphatically he skips the grin and lets his plane once again carry him away.

When a Flying Tiger does involve himself with the messy aftermath of combat, it is never on its own terms but always within a mythic code. Robert L. Scott Jr. describes one such scene in *God Is My Co-Pilot,* where the flyer involved is Tex Hill, one of Chennault's most reliable men throughout the AVG and USAAF periods. The occasion is a shootout over Hengyang, a very literal shootout in which the pilot of a Japanese Zero engages Tex Hill's P-40 in a terrifying head-on attack. The planes converge within the lines of each other's fire and disappear in a central explosion. From the clouds of fire and debris emerges Tex's Tomahawk, miraculously intact as the Zero plunges in flames to crash below. Preparing his readers for what will follow, Scott builds a convincing picture of Wild West imagery. Tex is so nicknamed, we learn, not simply because he's from that state but because his father has been chaplain to the Texas Rangers. He himself looks and acts the part of a cowboy if not a Ranger, long and lean with a loping gait only slightly encumbered by the Colt .45 revolver low-holstered at his side. The shoot-out itself has transpired just like a face-off in the streets of old-time Laredo. All of this embroidery is needed to justify what Tex Hill actually does when he lands and approaches the crash site:

> Tex's blond hair was blowing in the wind, his eyes were looking with venomous hate at the Jap, his jaw was set. I had

opened my mouth to congratulate him, for he had shot down two enemy ships that day, when I had a closer look at his eyes. . . . Tex strode over close to the fire and looked at the mutilated Jap where he had been thrown from the cockpit. Then, without a change of expression, he kicked the largest piece of Jap—the head and one shoulder—into the fire. I heard his slow drawl: "All right, mister—if that's the way you want to fight it's all right with me." (p. 176)

The words are not those of an AVG pilot but of John Wayne, conveniently so, as Wayne had already appeared in *The Flying Tigers* as produced in Hollywood. But even more so these are the words and actions of an American folk figure, the frontier lawman who has been tried too hard and been pushed far, and who after killing his brutal enemy fair and square can be excused for expressing his feelings.

Yet there are plenty of times when animosity is expressed with a studied callousness rarely found in European theater descriptions. By the time of Donald S. Lopez's Army Air Force service with Chennault in China, the Flying Tigers had acquired more than just an attitude toward the Japanese. Unlike their earliest AVG predecessors who had to whip up hostile sentiments based on four-year-old newspaper accounts of the rape of Nanking and Chennault's characterization of the Chinese as helpless victims of systematic air raids, the latter-day Tigers could name colleagues shot in parachutes, tortured, and then butchered when captured and relate it all to the infamy of the Pearl Harbor attack. News from Bataan had been even worse, and listening to the arrogance of propaganda broadcasts from Tokyo was infuriating. Reading their accounts today, one is struck by the memoirists' ability to distance themselves so completely from any shared sense of humanity with their adversaries. After a supply convoy with horse-drawn equipment is machine-gunned into oblivion Lopez takes time in *Into the Teeth of the Tiger* to explain how such things could be done. "Probably because of our deep enmity toward the Japs," he considers, "no one ever expressed anything but satisfaction at the success of a mission like this, except that many pilots regretted having to kill the horses. Killing the men bothered no one" (p. 148). A current of racial distinction runs through books written at the time, where not only are the Japanese crudely denigrated but the Anglo-Indian and Anglo-Burmese women who became the flyers' girlfriends are dismissed with smug references to dark skin. In this respect Olga Greenlaw's *The Lady and the Tigers* reads awkwardly fifty years later in an American culture more sensitive to diversity. But it is instructive nonetheless to see such attitudes anticipating later conduct. Writing in 1942, for example, the author of *God Is My Co-Pilot* can take great pleasure in his first major bombing raid, yelling, "Okay, Hirohito—we have lots more where those came from!" while revelling in the vivid bursts on his Japanese target below (p. 27). In such a context, it is understandable how firebombing, controversial when used in the European theater against Dresden, became an accepted practice in the air war versus Japan. Indeed, Curtis LeMay was hailed for choosing it as the only effective method. But Robert L. Scott's feelings are even more suggestive of the future when they take the form of telling Chennault "how I wished I could press a button and kill all the Japanese, to end the war, so that we could all go home" (p. 220), a premonition of how the mass destruction of atomic warfare would in fact become the Allies' final measure.

In a desensitized climate, it is remarkable how Chennault's flyers were able to write as beautifully and as lyrically as they often did. They had little inspiration for nobility when it came to the enemy they fought, nor could they share immediate kinship with those they defended, such as motivated Battle of Britain pilots both in their fighting and in how they wrote about it. Even when it came to representing America in the war, there reflected a sense of abandonment. On December 6, 1941, on the eve of Pearl Harbor, R.T. Smith sits in Burma fuming over his confused role: "If the Wizards of Washington ever make up their minds what to do about the Japs maybe we'll know when the hell to go to China" (p. 142). Not that Japan's attack made things for the AVG any easier. On the balance, it made matters worse, with vital supplies now prioritized by regular service demands. On February 25, 1942, when he'd been at war for twice as long as his country, Charlie Bond could be comically bitter. "Heard a rumor today that an Axis submarine hit some coastal city in the States," he notes. "Good, maybe that'll wake 'em up at home" (p. 110). Chennault's *Way of a Fighter* has him quoting a March 17, 1942, cable to T.V. Soong, his representative in Washington, complaining that he's "completely discouraged [at the] War Department failure [to] take advantage [of] China opportunities for air offensive against enemy. After three and a half months" (p. 153). Yet the Colonel soldiered on, Smith and Bond kept flying, and they and the rest of the Flying Tigers continued accumulating details of a unique experience that at the time or later they'd transform into almost breathtaking literary language.

Consider Lopez, who just a chapter before had boasted how he and his colleagues could shoot up Japanese men and horses and pity only the horses. For a more properly abstract night mission his writing becomes almost lovingly aesthetic:

> Four jeeps were parked across the left side of the runway with their lights shining across the runway. The leaders of each two-man element used these to line up the takeoff, while the wingmen flew formation on the leaders. We flew with our running lights on and climbed straight ahead until above the mountains, then made one circle to form up and headed north. We climbed to about 12,000 feet and flew well west of the river and railroad running from Hengyang to Kweilin. It was quite beautiful, with the gently bobbing running lights and the soft blue-red glow of the exhaust stacks, and it became more beautiful as the sky lightened and the P-40s emerged from the darkness, first as silhouettes, then becoming whole airplanes bathed by the faint light of dawn. As soon as we could see well, we turned off our lights. This was the first time most of us had ever flown formation at night, and it was a strangely tranquil experience. (p. 165)

Or listen to Olga Greenlaw, elsewhere so quick to note if a local woman befriending the AVG were "a little too much on the dusky side for me," here at the same Hengyang base describing what it's like to be on the receiving end of a nighttime bomb attack:

> I remember most vividly one brilliant moonlight raid—twenty-

seven Japanese bombers looking like silver toys and in perfect formation until furious anti-aircraft fire scattered them and brought four tumbling to earth in streaks of red flame. They dropped their bombs haphazardly and as no one place seemed safer than another we all thought we would be killed. (p. 23)

Danger certainly does sharpen one's attention, mortal danger making one all the more responsive to physical detail. In truth, physical details seem all that these writers notice, the moment's harsh immediacy eclipsing any chance for rhetoric or other forms of verbal posturing. Later in the war, Charlie Olson flew escort missions with B-24s to Hong Kong, and in Wanda Cornelius and Thayne Short's *Ding Hao: America's Air War in China, 1937-1945* (1980) he describes the experience as it happens:

I mean you've trained for combat and all of this stuff, and finally the day arrives—your first encounter with the enemy. Your whole flight arrives down at Hong Kong, and all of a sudden "Varoom" come the Zeroes, the bombers' bomb-bay doors are open, bombs and belly tanks start raining down, and you drop your belly tank. And they start hollering, "Five o'clock, there's seven of them. Look at that slant-eyed . . . look out, here come those slant-eyed sons of bitches at three o'clock and there's about eight of them. Oh, look out somebody, My God. They got hit!" Then pretty soon you see a B-24 burning and spinning in, and you know it's full of men. Then two planes collide in midair—pieces of engine falling down, wheels flying through the air. Hell, finally a Zero goes by and you squeeze the trigger and nothing happens. You squeeze it and you don't even realize you have your gun switch off.

You don't know what to do. You're not even aware that you are there. There are no sounds. You're deaf from the time the engine starts back at the field. You're really deaf, you know, to normal sounds. You've got your phones on so when they talk you hear it because the sound is concentrated, but normally your only sensations are sight and touch.

The only message you get from the engine is vibration. You don't hear if the engine is missing. You don't hear it, you feel it. You feel the vibrations through the stick, through the throttle quadrant, through your feet on the rudder pedals, and through your seat—the contact points with the machine itself.

The moment the thing misses three licks you feel it. You pick up the vibrations instantly when you lose rpm's. You pick it up instantly if you've got something else, if you've got a hunk of metal missing somewhere, a rip, a tear, or something in the metal. You can feel it. You know this on your first contact because you've learned this through your training, how the plane normally feels and flies.

But you are overcome by the vastness of it all only once— the first contact. After that you're conscious and you know it's going to be hell to pay and you know people are going to be hurt. I mean that's part of the game. I mean you know people are going to get killed. You expect that, I mean—you just hope it isn't you. (pp. 408-9)

As Lopez and Greenlaw foreground color, light, and other aspects of atmosphere, Olson recasts his experience in terms of its rhythms. All three writers privilege the reader's senses, just as their own ability to sense the adventure was sharpened to an acute sense of perception.

Writers bring their own personalities to the task, and descriptions of common aviation phenomena can be as distinct as their authors. Take the simple matter of contrails, those lines of writing in the sky that signify an aircraft's presence. For Pappy Boyington in *Baa Baa Black Sheep*, they are mundane, even when the survival of Rangoon is at stake: "During one of these battles the air above us would become so full of vapor trails the sky gave the appearance of some giant bird leaving chicken tracks in the barnyard mud" (p. 61). Robert L. Scott, prone to give his books titles such as *God Is My Co-Pilot* and *The Day I Owned the Sky*, reads contrails differently, admiring in the first work how their "criss-crossing vapor paths . . . almost covered the sky in a cloud" yet remained discernable as records of action, including the inscription of "darker lines that could have been smoke paths where ships had burned and gone down to destruction" (p. 230). An irony of such memoirs is how combat has its aesthetic qualities, such as when Scott observes a bomber formation at night and sees "their exhausts, looking like ten bushel-baskets of fire" (p. 178), or when Lopez, about to be bombed himself, studies the Nakajima Ki.48 Lilys bearing down on his field: "Although I had studied them in silhouette and model for the past year, seeing them in full scale, approaching with their bomb doors open, was quite a different thing," he appreciates, momentarily disregarding danger to note how "the dark and light green mottled camouflage and the enormous red ball insignias gave them an ominous beauty" (p. 84). Even crashes have their stark beauty, as does one near the home field where the ground crew can observe what the narrator of *God Is My Co-Pilot* describes. Under attack from a lone fighter, one bomber is hit, takes fire, and spins away. A second explodes and turns over, spectacular in the nighttime sky. "The third one tried to turn, seemed to hang for seconds against the full moon, then dove in flames in a pitch that got steeper and steeper," he writes. "Several thousand feet below our level it exploded and burning petrol fell with it. The light of the three burning bombers combined with the brilliant moonlight to make the night like day" (p. 179).

In the thick of combat, language further animates the action—nose guns thudding like twin jackhammers ripping up pavement, incendiary tracers from a bomber sailing out like burning pieces of paper being dropped from the tail, enemy fighters being strafed on the ground and seeming to shake themselves to pieces as the attacker's bullets strike. But then the adventuresome young men who flew for Chennault were given to speaking in ways that could animate anything. Gerhard Neumann cites an example in his *Herman the German* as part of his introduction to the AVG in Kunming. Walking down a city street with several pilots, the group comes up behind what the author describes as "an attractive Chinese girl in a tight silk dress." A volunteer from Texas, however, puts it another way, exclaiming to Neumann's great confusion that "I'd like to bite her in the ass and let her drag me to death!" (p. 81).

Most of all, the care taken in writing this group of memoirs reflects their authors' appreciation of how unique their perspective was. With previous knowledge of the Far East often limited to what they'd read from Kipling's poems, fulsome romance novels, and even high-adventure comic strips, they appreciated what they were experiencing in a strange land fighting a new war America had yet to acknowledge as deserving close attention, attention that they alone were able to pay. As such, their narratives joined a little known but now emerging tradition of accounts by people in the flying business taking note of this region created as it were for their careers. Paul Frillmann, who before the war had been a missionary to China, knew well the sense of living on the edge, and when despite the AVG's and RAF's valiant efforts at defense the Burmese capital begins to falter, his eye for detail and feeling for the rhythms of existence let him capture the experience perfectly:

> For a few days the streets were lined with merchant trucks unloading, then they drove off and Rangoon was noticeably more deserted. Later I was sorry I was too busy to keep a journal of the steps in the city's death, but as I remember it was the buses and taxis that disappeared next, driven off full of refugees. Then the newspapers died, the restaurants closed, the street-sweepers and garbage-collectors disappeared, and the street lights and electric signs went dark. Then the electricity itself was turned off, so was the water. The telephones went dead and the police deserted. In Hankow we had always known many of us were neutral; so was part of the city, but in Rangoon nothing was safe. Each day the emptying streets slipped back a little farther toward jungle. (p. 109)

When the last devastating bombings come and a city falls, an aviator's view is even more privileged. At the start of Japan's war against China, Royal Leonard found himself making an approach to Nanking in the last hours before its fall, a sight that inspires some of the best descriptive language in *I Flew for China*:

> The death of a city is always an awesome sight from the air, great in its sadness. I have seen it many times. The sign is always the same, infallible and changeless. Look only at the lights. When a city is in full health, free of war, its lights are gay and bright, even in China. There is no fear in its illumination. From the air it is the most cheering and inspirational sight possible. But when it begins to be frightened the lights, somehow, become dull. Perhaps the householders step outside, switching off their lights, blowing out lamps and candles, the better to see the sky. Perhaps the merchants close up. When the last convulsion comes there is only blackness before the burning. The whole effect is as if the city were a theater just before a grim performance. The house lights go slowly down,

and then the thick dark. It may take weeks and days for this to happen. It makes no difference. Time is immaterial to anyone who has been as familiar with a city as I had been for months with Nanking.

Flying now, on this night of its dying, I saw Nanking's lights dim, shrouded in smoke and glimmering like will-o-the-wisps. Parts of the city were already dead in darkness. (pp. 190-91)

This is at almost the same moment Chennault, only recently put to work as Chiang Kai-shek's chief air advisor, is preparing to fly himself out of his employer's doomed capital. Here, in Chennault's *Way of a Fighter*, the writing style complements Leonard's:

I went out to the bomb-cratered airfield at midnight to gas and warm up the Hawk for flight. The sound of its roaring engine momentarily drowned out the angry growling of the guns, hourly growing louder. I taxied out to the end of the runway in the dark and waited with engine idling and hand on the throttle for the first faint streaks of dawn to break over the city wall and light my take-off. The air-raid warning net had crumbled before the Japanese armies. Enemy fighters were on the prowl. Shells were bursting near the field. As I roared over the city wall, the sun was just beginning to rise, casting a pink glow over the stricken city, which gradually changed to a prophetic bloody red. (p. 60)

When the flyers of Chennault's American Volunteer Group left a more secure China five years later in July 1942, conditions of departure did not seem appropriate for such valedictory sentiments. Fighting the Japanese had inspired their best writing, but in the way they had to leave AVG service their enemy became the United States Army Air Force. The matter concerned when and how they might be made part of this new force. The issue first presented itself with the news of Pearl Harbor. In England, the American volunteers in the RAF flying as the three Eagle Squadrons reacted quickly, sending representatives to the U.S. Embassy in London on December 8, 1941, with the offer of enlisting en masse. Ambassador John Winant phoned President Roosevelt, and though promises were made to accept them, nothing happened; it would be almost a year before the USAAF could establish any real presence in England, and in the meantime the Eagles, as RAF squadrons, were excellent for both propaganda and morale. Still eager to fight their own country's enemy, they next requested transfer to Singapore, where the RAF was desperate to hold off the Japanese. This request was turned down by the Royal Air Force itself, with Air Chief Marshal William Sholto Douglas declaring that the Far East was crumbling, Singapore was about to fall, and nothing out there merited squadrons being taken out of the first line at home. As it happened, the Eagles did not join the USAAF until September 29, 1942, when they were transferred into the Eighth Air Force's 4th Fighter Group, among which the individual pilots were soon dispersed to become its backbone as experienced flight and squadron leaders.

From their bases in China and Burma, members of the AVG felt the same patriotic promptings as did their cousins in the Eagle Squadrons. But from the start their motivations were overswept by a tide of politics and policy wrangles that made their own experience go sour. First, it was a surprising initiative from the British, who as America's new allies wanted the AVG to operate under RAF command. Chennault "opposed this transfer . . . stubbornly," as he recalls in his autobiography (p. 125), though as time went by his motives for doing so showed the influence of personal ambition: having run the show in China since its start, he wanted to continue in that capacity right through to the end, and his sole convincing reason for being able to do so was as the commander of the only effective unit in place. An independently intact AVG was his main asset, and so its immediate induction into either the USAAF or the RAF was nothing he wanted to encourage. Not that the Army Air Force was eager to have these men back in the ranks, accustomed as they had become to high pay, loose discipline, and the feeling of being superior to their former service colleagues. With their leader's reputation of having been the black sheep of military aviation and a large number of old enemies just now assuming high staff and command positions themselves, the prospect of any sort of integration with the regular services looked to be an extremely problematic matter.

As it happened, the business of the AVG and the USAAF developed even worse than could have been imagined. Whereas in England the Eagle Squadrons and the 4th Fighter Group melded with the greatest ease and best publicity possible, newsreel cameras cranking as the Union Jack was lowered, the Stars and Stripes raised, and the top figures from each command smartly saluting the hand over, the scene in China played out through months of curiosity, confusion, worry, insult, anger, and eventual bitterness, with petty retribution on the military's part closing an unfortunate action that some commentators say broke Chennault's heart, for the Old Man was to continue the fight he had pioneered with just a few of the young flyers he'd nurtured and placed in a primary position to fight America's air war in the Far East. Many say he felt abandoned and betrayed—first by the politically careerist Air Corps, then by an America unwilling to see war imminent in the East, and finally by almost all of his own men.

Charlie Bond's diary is a good index to these developments, because of his longer prewar service and continuing hopes for a regular commission and lifetime career in the Air Force. When on December 16, 1941, the RAF sends a Blenheim to take Chennault to conferences in Rangoon, Bond wonders naively "if plans are being laid to induct us into the U.S. Army Air Corps" (p. 55) when in fact the AVG leader was being asked to put his men in British service. On January 2, 1942, he hears a rumor that Lieutenant General George Brett, USAAF chief in the Southwest Pacific, is talking about induction. "This has started lengthy discussions throughout the outfit," Bond notes. "The general consensus is to stay the way we are, but I doubt if we will. I am willing to go back into the Air Corps right now if they will give me a regular commission" (p. 69).

Here, less than a month after Pearl Harbor, Bond reveals what would be the flaw in AVG thinking. It doesn't matter that his career plans set him apart from the group's attitude, which in itself was by no means unpatriotic—in England the Eagle Squadrons as well wanted to enter the USAAF as a unit and continue to fly that way; even giving up their

Spitfires was regretted, and when soon after transfer they were split up to distribute their experience throughout the fledgling 4th Fighter Group there was much disappointment. From the military's point of view, one can see how such ambitions as the Eagles' and the AVG's are impractical. An air force must operate uniformly to the same standards and with interchangeable parts; letting a group of three squadrons continue with its unique practices would be detrimental to the larger group's purpose. In their hearts the Eagles knew this, and the members of the AVG must have known it, too. But Chennault's men made the mistake of thinking they were dealing with the Army Air Force from a position of strength, whether it be to maintain unit integrity or negotiate for regular commissions. As it turned out, they had no power beyond the threat they'd held over Chennault himself: to quit and go home. And when they did that, the military would make things miserable for them, indeed.

As January ends, however, prospects as reported in Bond's diary are still looking good. Sandy Sandell, close to the center as a squadron leader, tells Bond that induction is assured, with Chennault's individual recommendations setting each man's rank. This puts Bond in a very good mood, and when later in the day he lands at Rangoon and sees a USAAF B-17E bomber parked across the field he's prompted to exclaim "Damn, it looks good!" (p. 81). Yet nothing happens for the next two months, beyond the deterioration of both equipment and spirit, the resignations and firings of more pilots, and the increase in tension that would lead to the April mutiny over morale missions and low-level escorts. On March 26 Bond describes a meeting called by Chennault to discuss induction—after a full winter of rumors and speculations, the first formal consideration of this crucial matter. Bond asks about the chances of getting regular commissions; Chennault dismays him by stating that there's been no talk about that whatsoever. Other pilots say they'd like to either go home immediately or stay in China only to fulfill their AVG contracts as civilians; Chennault implies he can fill their vacancies with replacements. From this very unsatisfactory discussion only one clear point emerges, that "there was no doubt that the Old Man's first and foremost desire is to keep us together as his AVG" (p. 146)—*his* AVG, readers will note.

From this point on, and especially in the wake of the abortive mutiny, alternatives come up in Bond's considerations. On April 11 a DC-3 comes through, flown by an old service buddy from MacDill Field, who says any ex-AVG pilots would be snapped up quickly by Pan American Airways for $750 per month, more than thrice USAAF officer pay and as good as most were making with Chennault. "I am making a mental note of this," Bond confides. "Things are still uncertain for my future" (p. 152). On April 19 he's given a direct job offer, $800 monthly to fly for CNAC, the China National Aviation Corporation—another paramilitary operation paying its civilian contract employees hefty bonuses that let them clear $1,200 per month. "It is enticing, I have to admit, but I turned it down for the time being," Bond confides. "I asked him to let me think about it for a while" (p. 157).

As part of Chennault's headquarters staff, Olga Greenlaw had a closer feel for what was going on and a larger perspective when it came to the national interest. As early as mid-February she could note the increasingly frequent visits from military personnel and take a different view toward it than prevailed among the AVG. "With the coming of so many American Army officers, the boys were certain we would be inducted," she writes. "That, they didn't want, and for that reason they resented the presence of the American Army officers. I didn't. I thought we needed the moral support of the American Government and liked to see the interest that was being taken in our group" (p. 140). But her broader view neglected the different interests among the pilots. Some, like Charlie Bond, saw the more rarified doings of general officers as guiding lights of policy. Others, such as Pappy Boyington, thought policy was politics and that politics stunk. Yet in *Baa Baa Black Sheep* he succumbs to military politics of the lowest order, that of interservice rivalry, vented in almost the same breath as his condemnation of careerism:

> At this particular period the AVG, as small as it was,
> happened to represent the only citizens of the United States
> who had not only held their own but had gone on to create a
> most enviable record. Their success, not defeat, was by far the
> greatest in the war to date. So, a high-ranking general in the
> Air Corps recognized personal glory to be within easy grasp if
> he could but annex this group of civilians to his command.
> One other minor little detail had to occur to make this
> proposed annexation complete before this general would be
> able to boost his stock and yet give a legal appearance. All of
> the AVG pilots had to be inducted, as it was so aptly worded
> for lack of better words, into the Air Corps. I personally
> considered this to be the rottenest kind of a farce, for, though
> Chennault himself was a dyed-in-the-wool Air Corps man, he
> had earned his reputation with a crew of pilots of which better
> than 50 percent had come from Uncle Sam's Navy and Marine
> Corps. (pp. 78-89)

Chennault, of course, was far from dyed in the wool; to borrow a different part of Boyington's extended metaphor, he was the black sheep of the Air Corps and had been so since Pappy wore diapers. As renegades together, Army, Navy, and Marine flyers had gotten along well in the AVG, though their distribution into squadrons had partly reflected their native branches. But the idea of naval aviators going back into the regular service as Army Air Force flyers grated against Boyington's deepest feelings, and perhaps for good reason. Pappy had been shamed in the Marine Corps, and it was there that he wanted to recover his good name. The way he did it, by running the Black Sheep Squadron in a manner reminiscent of Chennault's way with the AVG, could never have happened in a branch of service where he was an alien, a rival much as he was seeing the Air Corps now.

In *Tonya*, Boyington sets this unhappy affair in exclusively political terms. The high-ranking general eager for a career boost is a fictitious version of Clayton S. Bissell, here called Gen. B.S. Sittel, all puns intended. Although his argument against letting the AVG retain its contractual status while fighting alongside units of the USAAF holds water— that it would be impossible to run a war where one pilot would serve under military discipline for low service pay while another earned so much more, with bonuses for kills as well—this character's disposition is so venal as to overshadow any moneymaking by the AVG; in emphasizing this trait, Boyington alludes not just to Bissell's wartime stinginess with supplies but his later shame in being forced out of the service for embezzlement, a story Robert L. Scott recounts firsthand in *The Day I Owned the Sky* as a member of the Air Force's board of review. Though more formidable a man, the stand-in for Chennault fares no better, for at the end of *Tonya* he's shamed when his pilots learn he has lied about their induction as a way of keeping them counted as his own forces while he maneuvers for command authority in the USAAF. Although his own exploits make Pappy Boyington an unlikely spokesman for ideals, his distaste for the politics of the induction affair represents what by the end was an almost universal feeling.

Diary entries by two of the AVG's three Bob Smiths express the noncareerist but also unpoliticized feelings of most Flying Tigers. On January 25, 1942, R.T. Smith mentions that there's a "rumor running around about the Army taking over our group," but moves on to a more interesting topic: a hunting trip tomorrow. Footnoting this page as he prepares his *Tale of a Tiger*, R.T. recalls that for months nobody really knew what was going to happen; "Meanwhile, all we wanted was to be left alone and allowed to continue the fight under the terms of our original agreement, though we knew that this could not continue indefinitely" (p. 198). Much later in the process, radioman Robert M. Smith expresses a similar detachment in his entry for *With Chennault in China* on May 4, when terms for reenlistment had been proposed: "Radiograms were sent by our headquarters to all radio station masters offering them technical sergeant. The consensus was a definite no. We all want to go home" (p. 83).

It was just when the AVG's eagerness to join and fight cooled down that the Army Air Force finally made its move to take them into the fold. On May 7, 1942, the Commander-in-Chief, Franklin D. Roosevelt himself, sent a special message to the volunteers asking them to stay in China at least until a regular wing could arrive to take their place. "Most of the guys think lightly of the idea," Charlie Bond reports. "All want to return to the States as soon as possible. I am not sure how this is going to turn out" (p. 175). By May 11 he is noting "more and more talk about an official induction of the AVG on July 4" and countering it with the sentiment that "most of the guys just want to go home" (p. 176).

Finally, on May 21, 1942, the Army Air Force came to address Chennault's men. Its representative was the worst possible choice, General Clayton S. Bissell, famous from the ubiquitously innocent Chinese greeting "Piss on Bissell!" and having already taken shape in Pappy Boyington's imagination as "General B.S. Sittel." Meeting him that day, R.T. Smith is able to gauge that the man "had all the charm of a cobra" (p. 318). In *Flying Tiger: A Crew Chief's Story* (1996), Frank S. Losonsky charges that "the Air Corps made a serious mistake sending Bissell to recruit. His pitch had little effect. He was rude, arrogant, and projected an attitude of indifference toward myself and my comrades. The man turned us off." Although Bissell would be staying around to conduct interviews, Losonsky realizes from the start that "most of us felt we'd been shafted and had no desire to serve under his command" (p. 94). Even Charlie Bond, who would become a major general in the postwar United States Air Force, leaves the meeting "steaming mad" (p. 178) and gathers with his friends to "cuss a lot" and hear their intentions "to go back to the States and take the chance of being drafted" (p. 179). For Bond himself, the moment is the saddest in *A Flying Tiger's Diary:*

> I haven't made up my mind. I lie awake until the wee hours of the morning trying to decide. Here I am within reach of what I have come over here for. It has turned out exactly as I had thought: I would get combat experience by the time the U.S. got into the war and be in a perfect position to parlay that into a regular commission when the time came to integrate the AVG into the USAAC. In the meantime I would have saved up some money. And now my key and most important goal is going down the drain. What to do? (p. 179)

What had Bissell done to so infuriate the men—every one of them, from Chennault loyalists and future Air Force career officers to the most carefree renegades in the group, from pilots to ground crewmen and technicians? The problem was with both his bad news and the way he had chosen to convey it. He was not there to ask for the volunteer's reenlistments; instead, he informed them that they had no choice, that they were going to be inducted into the USAAF whether they liked it or not. If they refused, lots of luck getting back to the States—no transport service, either a part of the military or one doing business with it, would sell them passage. Nor would Pan Am, CNAC, or any other airline operating overseas or in the United States hire them—he'd see to that (and by having Chennault write the airlines with a personal appeal, he did). Once they did get home, a draft board notice would be waiting to put them in the front lines of the infantry as buck privates. Yet even if they did submit to induction, there'd be no sweet deals: just minimum rank, reserve rather than regular commissions (meaning no Air Force future after the war), and no furlough before active service in the USAAF's new China command.

Making it all the worse was Bissell's attitude toward the AVG. These were not heroes he was addressing—they were the rabble who needed to be whipped and hammered into military shape. They were not combat-weary fighters who'd been struggling at odds in terrible conditions at the mercy of deteriorating equipment—they were playboys of the air, "flying fools" as the hometown newspapers liked to call them or, worse yet, the swashbuckling adventurers pictured so often in *Time* and *Life* and the newsreels that in the meantime had only failures in the regular service to report. Above all they were mercenaries, fighting by their own rules (or none at all) for fun and profit. It was probably the unruliness that bothered Bissell most of all, for spit-and-polish by the rulebook were his specialty; cases of blanco and brasso and typewriter ribbons sometimes outweighed the ammunition he requisitioned for his command. And so his approach to the men of the AVG was especially harsh. Anything he had to say to them came with the voice of iron authority; whatever his listeners asked of him was shrugged off as being impossible because of rules, regulations, and red tape—

just the things that had driven many of these men out of the service and into Chennault's employ.

Yet after all of this, many if not most of the volunteers would have stayed had only General Bissell made them feel welcome. Almost every memoirist's account of his personal interview reads the same: not just being refused minimal courtesies but being rudely cut off even before asking. Frank Losonsky's experience replicates what they all went through and represents the group's sentiments:

> I remember the 27th [of May] well. It was one of the few direct times I talked to General Chennault. He called us in, one at a time. I told the General I wanted to fly. Chennault didn't have a chance to reply. General Bissell spoke up and said "Look the General doesn't have time to give you a recommendation to go to flying school." I replied, "But that's what I want you to do. I have flying experience, and I'd like to go to flight school." Bissell replied, "Stay here or else when you get home you will be drafted." I told him I'd take my chances with the draft. It was over in 4 minutes. I would have stayed had they given me flight school, a commission, or the promised thirty day leave. (p. 95)

Did the Army Air Force really want Chennault's men at all? For publicity purposes for the folks back home they surely had to ask, and a wonderful transfer ceremony such as happened with the Eagles four months later in England would have been a great boost for morale. But from geopolitics and larger strategy to the most personal of animosities, China and the AVG were different from England and the Eagle Squadrons. England was an old and stable ally, linked to the United States by language, culture, history, tradition, and complementary national aims. China was a new factor in the world, and far from stable; American policy makers were already arguing over whom to support, Chiang's Nationalists or the Communists emerging under Mao Tse-tung, a debate that would unsettle U.S. conduct toward China during the war and make larger trouble for postwar times. Strategically, this was no longer an ignored or forgotten theater, but the Allies' firm agreement was that in terms of defeating enemies Germany, not Japan, came first, so prime attention stayed directed to England's and not China's war. Then there was the matter of Chennault's standing with his former service. Deep down, he didn't want the Air Corps, and the Air Corps didn't want him. In the aftermath of Pearl Harbor he fought the notion of USAAF induction as stubbornly as he rejected having the RAF take over his command. Only when it became clear that his sole chance of keeping a leadership role in China depended on the AVG did he submit to the idea of assimilation, wisely getting his general's stars before his men knew what was happening. "Why were the Flying Tigers disbanded if they were doing so well?" Gerhard Neumann asks in *Herman the German.* "Because Chennault was boycotted by the U.S. War Department. No replacement aircraft, no ammunition and no spare parts arrived for him in China to support his tiny volunteer group of 253 men and two nurses. Many Air Corps generals in the States were jealous of the former schoolteacher and retired Army Air Corps captain who had become a world hero" (p. 93). Finally, and as Neumann had to agree, the Tigers and newly trained service personnel would make for an uncomfortable if not impossible mix, radically different as they were. Even Erik Shilling, given a rare attractive offer of major's rank and a smoothly unhassled interview, could see the truth of things when "as a parting question I asked Bissell what my chances would be of continuing in the Air Corps after the war." As noted in Shilling's *Destiny,* "His answer was blunt and to the point with an emphatic 'NONE.' It was not that he knew me, but only that I was a member of the AVG." So defined, Shilling reacts in character, standing up and saying "You can damn well shove it, Colonel" (p. 190), even in the moment's heat getting in a dig by addressing Bissell by his permanent rather than acting rank. As for how the group was approached, Shilling reports that "Almost to a man, the Flying Tigers I have talked to about Bissell's induction speech feel the same way as I did. That the intent was to discourage the AVG's induction into the military rather than encourage it" (p. 191).

It is hard to imagine any of the American Volunteer Group, other than the five exceptional pilots who accepted commissions, doing well in a China air war being run by the military. Chennault himself would struggle for three long years, not just with Bissell in terms of supply but with General Stilwell about strategy. The type of AVG energy that had brought these men to China a year ago now motivated them toward similarly independent approaches, whether it be further adventuring with CNAC or petitioning generals, senators, and the President himself for a regular commission, as did the indefatigable Charlie Bond. "We had been out of step with our complacent, isolationist country the year before, when we volunteered," Paul Frillmann realizes in *China: The Remembered Life*. "Now we were out of step again, when the conventional thing was to rush to the colors" (p. 158).

One heroic act prevented the AVG's story in China from closing on a thoroughly sour note. When June ended with only five pilots and twenty-two ground crewmen agreeing to join the Army Air Force and begin regular combat as the 23rd Fighter Group, Chennault realized that July 4, 1942, would dawn with an extremely vulnerable unit asking to be wiped out by the Japanese. To augment this number and the handful of USAAF people just beginning to arrive, he made a seemingly impossible request: that as many of the AVG who could please stay on for an extra two weeks to make the transition something other than absolute chaos. To their enduring credit, a surprising nineteen pilots and thirty-six ground crew members agreed—becoming for the first time literal volunteers, making a sacrifice for their successors, for their country, and most of all for Claire Chennault himself. Charlie Bond was one of them, cursing his conscience for making him do it. But he did, and fortunately survived. Two pilots did not, including the just-married and father-to-be Johnny Petach, whose pregnant wife, the former nurse Emma "Red" Foster, had to suffer the same travel indignities as the rest of the departing Tigers as they struggled to make their way home. When born, her daughter was named "Claire."

In later years, there was much bitterness to be recalled. In *Tiger Tales* (1984) Milt Miller, a bombardier with Chennault's subsequent Fourteenth Air Force in China, mentions a "good old days" conversation with his leader a decade later: "I'll never forget how, at one point in our discussion, he paused, his eyes hardened, his jaw stiffened, and he quietly said: 'I never had trouble with the Japanese. It was those bastards in Washington I had to worry about'" (p. 109). The hard eyes, the stiffly jutted jaw, the posture of defiance— Miller's words fit almost every photograph taken of Claire Chennault, especially the portrait poses such as the one that appears opposite the title page of the appropriately titled *Way of a Fighter,* as if this complaint is what was on his mind. In *Flying Tiger: Chennault of China,* Robert L. Scott expands this sentiment to the AVG at large, writing in 1959 that "for the men who flew for Chennault there remains to this day a bitterness that has been and will be felt for a long, long time, a bitterness such as must have been rarely, if ever, felt by soldiers who fought in other theaters of war." Why so? "For they saw the human jealousies and ignorance kill their own friends and, worse, render their sacrifices useless" (p. 236).

Useless might well be the men's feeling, but more adequate measures of the Flying Tigers' usefulness exist. Even in the least heroic terms, the mercenary economics by which they were recruited and for which many of them served, their cost effectiveness was remarkable, if not to say even fabulous. At the time and for half a century afterward, the American Volunteer Group was, over six months of combat, credited with 296 kills—the number confirmed by the Chinese government and paid for as bonuses to the respective pilots. In his exhaustive and authoritative *Flying Tigers: Claire Chennault and the American Volunteer Group,* historian Daniel Ford revises this total down to the level of between 110 and 120 Japanese planes lost to the AVG in Burma, Thailand, and China. "The toll in lives was far higher," Ford adds, noting that these planes carried more men, operated over enemy territory, and rarely held parachutes, making for losses in excess of four hundred men (p. 370). For AVG losses, three pilots died in training and twenty-two others were killed in combat, captured, or missing. Material losses were much higher—eighty-six AVG planes never flew again—but then nobody else had wanted them in the first place. In dollars alone, China had bought in for $9.3 million and sold out (to the USAAF when it assumed responsibility for what remained on July 4, 1942) for $3.5 million credit on its Lend-Lease account. As Ford calculates, "the net cost to China for the services of the American Volunteer Group was $5.8 million for aircraft and $3 million for salaries and combat bonuses, or a bit more than $75,000 for each Japanese plane destroyed." Was this a good deal for China? Yes, because "it was one of the rare instances in modern warfare where the instrument of destruction cost less than the objects destroyed" (p. 374). Budgets of ten times as much and more would be required for the USAAF to take over the job.

Beyond numbers was the AVG's psychological importance. Though they themselves did not defeat the Japanese, they accomplished several actions that undoubtedly contributed to the success of later forces in achieving that victory. In their very first combat operation, on December 20, 1941, they caused such havoc among Japanese bombers over Kunming that such attacks, which had been a fact of life for the previously defenseless Chinese, ceased altogether. Then, just a few days later, another AVG squadron undertook the defense of Rangoon, holding off the fall of that city for months beyond what the RAF alone, with its inferior equipment, could have done. Then, in May of 1942, its interdiction of the Japanese column advancing through the Salween Gorge stopped the potential invasion of Chiang's last secure portion of China. After Pearl Harbor, there had been rumors that China might make a separate peace. This would have left the Japanese free to concentrate more of their strength against India and onward as far as Egypt, where they would have joined forces with the German Afrika Korps. Had that happened, the question of which war came first and which came last would have been immaterial.

As happened, the AVG held China in the war until regular forces could be sent there. Its successor, the 23rd Fighter Group, maintained the healthy success ratio against just as long odds, destroying over a thousand enemy aircraft while losing less than two hundred of its own. As Robert L. Scott writes in *The Day I Owned the Sky,* "I feel honored to have been the first group commander, and despise Bissell for denying it so many other good men; had he been even half-way diplomatic, as General Arnold must have expected him to be, the entire AVG might have remained" (p. 74-75). But even so, they would have faced the same old obstacles of poor equipment, insufficient supplies, command hassles (made worse by Bissell and Stilwell), and conflicting strategies from different camps in Washington. Chennault himself had to carry on the same way, writing President Roosevelt when all else failed and threatening publicity stunts that would have damaged the Army immensely had they not backed down. There is no doubt whatsoever that neither the volunteer nor regular Flying Tigers could have operated successfully without him.

And so the fight at odds in China is not only remembered as a war conducted by iconically striking figures, but after close study turns out to have actually happened that way. Not only at the time but for decades afterward, Pappy Boyington and Robert L. Scott would represent the alternately devilish and pious sides of such iconography, but the most impressive (and impressively effective) figure remains Claire Chennault himself. At the Trident Conference, the single time his superiors made the mistake (for them) of letting Chennault return to North America and take part in strategy discussions, he caught the eye of Britain's chief representative, Prime Minister Winston Churchill. "Who is that man?" Churchill asked, indicating the hawklike visage of the AVG commander so apparent among the U.S. delegation. When told, the Prime Minister simply growled, "I'm glad he's on our side."

The RAF's Less than Finest Hour

− • − The American Volunteer Group's first view of the Royal Air Force in Burma was a revealing one: there was no one to be seen. The scene repeated itself as the three successive travel groups of AVG men arrived in Burma after their ocean crossing from the States. Before traveling up to the Kyedaw airfield outside Toungoo where they would undertake their training, Chennault's recruits all had at least part of a day if not more to explore Rangoon and learn what this new place was like. There were sights and sounds, smells and textures galore, all of them exotic, from the colorfully dressed Burmese to the wide range of novel goods being sold by the mostly Indian shopkeepers. But during these midday adventures, there were no English people in evidence. That was something to be learned as well: that during the heat of day the British kept to their clubs for prolonged lunches or returned home for a nap.

The picture is drawn best by R.T. Smith in the commentary that prepares his diary, *Tale of Tiger,* for readers a generation hence. On this first day in country he has purchased the blank diary itself, a guidebook to Burma, and two tins of Players cigarettes. But before trying to comprehend Burma he organizes a perspective of the people who rule it, who at this moment of the day are not on station at the helm:

> Here, as in Singapore, the British residents lived at a very leisurely pace in comparative luxury. Most had spacious, comfortable housing provided by the government, in the case of civil employees of the crown, or by the many companies engaged in commerce. Native servants could be hired for the equivalent of fifteen or twenty dollars per month, and most British households had at least three or four of them. Food and clothing were plentiful and inexpensive, and considerable time off was allowed for vacations in the highlands of northern Burma during the hottest part of the year, which must surely include the present. Later we learned that much the same applied to the British in India and other colonies, and it was easy to see why so many chose to accept employment in the Far East. This far from the action and the struggle going on in Europe, it was hard to believe that England was fighting for her life against Nazi Germany. (p. 57)

This sense of ease and isolation from danger becomes a recurrent theme not just in the AVG memoirs with respect to the British but in nearly all of the local RAF narratives as well. Everyone from the air officer commanding to the lowest ranked pilot officer in these colonially based squadrons might well plead for more commitment to the war effort. But until war eventually came to localities such as Hong Kong, Singapore, and Rangoon, resident English populations refused to acknowledge any danger. When Japan did make its move, any amount of local consternation was too late, for an embattled Britain still too weak to launch a major offensive at home was in no position to send more than token forces to its far outposts of empire.

Looking further back, historians argue that the fall of Singapore and Rangoon had been ordained almost twenty years before, when the defenses prepared for each city were oriented exclusively toward the sea. This refusal to believe that an enemy army could advance down the Malay peninsula (to capture Singapore) and across Thailand (to threaten Rangoon) invited a Japanese strategy that made victory for the emperor almost a foregone conclusion. By December 1941, London must have known this, for no effort to save its colonies seemed worth contemplating. But from a Flying Tiger's point of view, the lack of a serious attitude was quite apparently a local fact of life. On December 22, for example, when R.T. Smith and his squadron had already been sent back to Rangoon to patrol against expected Japanese bombers—for a raid that would in fact come the very next day— the young American pilot still finds everything in the city functioning as usual, with no evidence whatsoever of concern for war. When Smith stops at a jewelry store to pick up the gold signet ring he's ordered, the British manager refuses to take cash payment, saying he'll bill the flyer at the end of the month. "Little did either of us know that before that time the store would be in ruins and the city evacuated," Smith indicates in a footnote to his original entries for that day. "I still owe somebody for that ring, which I wear to this day" (p. 158). Even after two weeks of bombing, the city remained ill prepared to deal with hostilities. On January 6, 1942, radioman Robert M. Smith comments on this in his own diary, *With Chennault in China.* "The AVG were ready for war. We have been in intensive training since August," he rightfully boasts. "The British at Rangoon were not. They were poorly organized. There was no food for the AVG or British pilots. For three days their rations were bread and beer. They had butter on the bread for one breakfast" (p. 53).

Regard for the King's forces in Burma ran no higher at the head of AVG command. In his own memoirs, *"I've Seen the Best of It,"* Joseph W. Alsop replays an early staff meeting between his boss and the local hierarchy to clarify why Chennault "had no great liking for the British" (p. 179). The gathering is characterized by the high commissioner's drowning of defeatism in a tide of the largest gin gimlets Joe Alsop has ever seen; it is characteristic not only of this Washington insider's chauvinism but also of his appreciation for Chennault's staying power that the AVG leader is portrayed as the only one to resist drifting off to lotus-eating land. In his *Way of a Fighter,* Chennault regrets that the battle for Burma "was a disaster that nearly knocked China out of the war and sowed bitter seeds of dissension among the new British, Chinese, and American allies. The most tragic aspect of that bloody campaign was the utter lack of Allied unity." Here the blame is apportioned equally, the British thinking only of India (as a more securable dominion) while the top-ranking American military men made the Chinese feel equally abandoned by dealing with them "as a frontier cavalry commander of 1870 handled a tribe of friendly but untrustworthy Indians" (p. 140). Yet others on Chennault's staff were prone to blame the British, including Olga Greenlaw, AVG diarist and wife of the commander's chief-of-staff who with her husband had become something of an old hand at the Far East. "We had seen enough of the smug complacency, lethargy and ostrich-like head-in-the-sand attitude of the French in Indo-China, the Siamese, the Dutch, and the British in Hong Kong, Singapore and Burma to be convinced that they, tragically too late, would discover that they were also at war," she rues in *The Lady and the Tigers*. Even though the AVG was present to augment their own RAF squadrons and the docks of Rangoon were piled high with the materials for fighting a very real war, "These people simply would not believe anything could or would happen" (p. 31).

Face to face, the attitude of the AVG pilots toward their RAF counterparts was only a bit less problematic. "My first impression is that they are sissified dainties," Charlie Bond records after he and his colleague share scotch and soda with the English flyers at their club. So much for "first opinions about the British fighter pilots," although "others say they are gutsy guys" (p. 81). Two weeks of contact with the enemy doesn't help, as on February 2, 1942, Bond is dismayed to learn that the crucial RAF base at Moulmein "was evacuated ahead of the incoming Japs. They said only sixteen hundred Japanese troops took the place" (p. 92). As many other pages of *A Flying Tiger's Diary* report Bond's AVG squadron succeeding against astronomical odds, the implication is clear. Before Pearl Harbor, some Americans chided the locals that they were doing nothing and expected the United States to stop the Japanese for them; after December 7, speakers of this persuasion, rude as they were, felt they had the evidence behind them.

Not helping relations was the fact that on November 19,

1941, well before the Rangoon operations, when the entire AVG was still in the thick of its training at Kyedaw Airfield near Toungoo, representative British and American flyers engaged in a dogfight. It was arranged on friendly terms, was not inspired by any test of competition on national grounds, and was of course conducted without any ammunition, the goal being simply to outmaneuver the mock adversary by getting position on his tail. Erik Shilling was the AVG pilot chosen, and in his *Destiny* he explains how the matter came up not as any rivalry with the RAF but because of an ongoing debate about the plane they flew. The Brewster Buffalo that the RAF's Burma squadrons operated was not only an American plane but had been used earlier by the U.S. Navy. Many of the AVG pilots were former Navy flyers, and some of them thought it a better fighter than the P-40s their leader had obtained. To settle the argument and also to relieve the stress of training with a bit of a sideshow, Chennault arranged to have an RAF pilot bring one up and face off against the AVG's equipment.

Shilling's account of the dogfight is fair and even complimentary. His opponent, a squadron leader named Brandt, was a Battle of Britain ace who had outfought Messerschmitt 109s, so the Brewster was in capable hands. Shilling, however, was able to outturn it by slanting their circle to a 45 degree plane. "Each time at the top of the turn, with the Brewster below, I would pull back hard on the stick, doing a one quarter turn spin cutting across the circle and gaining a little each time" (p. 112). Brandt has his own tricks, including dropping landing gear and flaps in the hopes Shilling will overshoot. But the American sees the flaps lowering and so pulls back on the stick rather than reducing power, gaining altitude as he loses speed and therefore staying ready to jump back on his adversary's tail. Each pilot is gifted and gets the best from his machine, with the better plane, the P-40, winning.

Unfortunately for RAF-AVG relations, this was not how the contest was perceived. In R.T. Smith's diary there is no sign that the author knows that the issue is an Army-Navy contest rather than an evaluation of the RAF. "Shilling beat him," Smith notes, "but we all agree the RAF guy did a lousy job of flying. Looked like he wasn't trying and he made some lousy mistakes" (p. 123). Charlie Bond puts it even more bluntly, saying "Shilling clobbered his opponent" (p. 40), sharing Frank Losonsky's sentiments as expressed in *Flying Tiger: A Crew Chief's Story* that, as far as the RAF plane went, "the P-40 whipped the hell out of it" (p. 63). Another contemporary account brought this news (and the attitude behind it) to the American public in the form of Robert B. Hotz's *With General Chennault: The Story of the Flying Tigers.* Published early in 1943 with title-page credit given for the assistance of three prominent AVG pilots (Paxton, Neale, Dupouy) and mentioning at the start that Hotz was presently serving under Chennault's command in China, this volume spoke with apparent authority. The message it conveyed exaggerated even further the (nonexistent) RAF-AVG rivalry by describing how bets were taken on the outcome, something no diary or subsequent memoir mentions. Yet the idea of a wagering contest, replete with boastful challenges, long odds, and exorbitant sums (400 Indian rupees, or $150, half a month's pay for the ground crewman putting up the cash) made the situation more exciting to report and more rewarding for American loyalties when Hotz concluded that "Shilling flew rings around the stubby Buffalo and the RAF pilot" (p. 107).

A year earlier, in 1942, the very first book on Chennault's AVG had prepared readers to be skeptical about their British allies, at least as far as conduct in the Far East was concerned. In *The Flying Tigers,* Russell Whelan strikes a different note than sounded by the many current volumes celebrating the glamor of RAF pilots in the Battle of Britain and the tenacious courage of Londoners surviving the Blitz; to him the term "British" means senseless regulation for regulation's sake in denial of any need for efficiency, much less wartime commitment, as he illustrates when the first AVG recruits arrive in Rangoon. These future heroes, Whelan notes, are in either civilian clothes or plain khaki without insignia, but what they see shocks every military bone in their bodies:

As their ship approached the city they were vividly reminded of their mission by the scene along the three-mile length of wharves, where storage yards and warehouses bulged with thousands of packing cases awaiting shipment by rail and road to the north. This was American lend-lease material, the lifeblood of fighting China.

They found upon inquiry that many of the packing cases had been standing there for weeks and months, while China clamored for the supplies, and clamored in vain. One of the reasons for this, they learned, was the British custom ruling that permitted clearance of any article only when every one of its kind mentioned in the bill of lading was present on the spot and accounted for. Hence, if the papers described a shipment of five thousand automobile truck tires, and ten of these were mislaid during an unloading, the other four thousand nine hundred and ninety gathered dust on the wharves until the missing ten turned up. If they remained missing, the four thousand nine hundred and ninety stayed where they were, thus serving the ends of red tape but not of nations and empires fighting for their lives. (pp. 38-39)

It is important to note that Whelan doesn't need to write his scene quite this way. He wants to tell about the hung-up supplies, but his choice of exposition is rhetorical. By having the AVG recruits perceive it, as their first sight in country, the effect is to stir American anger, their own and their readers'. Here they are, having come over from a country not yet at war to volunteer their services to a pair of nations already declared as belligerents in World War II; the mention of civilian clothes and no insignia is a reminder of this fact. But what of the belligerents? One, China, is cut off from desperately needed supplies by the criminally stupid practices of the other, Great Britain. Nor are these just "supplies," but rather American Lend-Lease material. Taxpayer dollars are being wasted, money paid by the same Americans back home reading Whelan's book. To drive the economic argument to its inflammatory conclusion, the author repeats the accounting figures four times over, each time spelling out the numbers to enhance their grating presence. By the time he writes the words "red tape" readers are well stirred up. With the reminder that people are "fighting for their lives" comes the appreciation that this spectacle is being viewed by a ship-load of young Americans who will soon be doing just that.

When the war does come to Rangoon, Whelan scores another critical point. True, the civilian government does a good job of putting out the first air raid's fires, as good as had been done by their compatriots in London. "But the British made one mistake of omission—the kind of mistake that loses battles and wars" (p. 64), for, as the author notes, they had forgotten to take care of the Indian coolies working on the docks, nearly all of whom promptly walked off the job and returned back home to the subcontinent. It was the type of oversight that happens in unseen emergencies, a contingency for which no regulations have been prepared. Yet plenty of other regulations remained, many of them operating in a way that kept the absent Indian workers from being quickly replaced. As Olga Greenlaw sighs in her own book that reached American readers in the still-impressionable year of 1943, "If you think [AVG attempts to overcome this] succeeded you are ignorant of the intricacies of British red tape as it existed in Burma at that time. All the lawyers in Philadelphia couldn't have whipped that problem" (p. 24).

Olga Greenlaw could also find fault with British fighting units, painting the first stroke in a portrait of noncooperation that would emerge from a wide range of Flying Tiger narratives. When the Japanese began bombing Rangoon in late December 1941, by which time the United States and the United Kingdom had become formal allies, each at war with the same opponents in the same places, she had only poor examples to cite in the official AVG diary, as reproduced in *The Lady and the Tigers:*

> No air raid signal was given at Mingaladon [the principal defending air base]. All ships were suddenly ordered off airdrome. No information of enemy prior to take-off was known. Three minutes after take-off radio orders were given: "ENEMY APPROACHING FROM EAST."—No co-operation was given by anti-aircraft guns—pilots report that it was practically nil and very inaccurate. Fourteen P-40's and sixteen Brewsters (RAF) joined the fight. There was no friendly support from nearby [RAF] airdromes. (p. 91)

In the operations room back at AVG headquarters, pilot Jack Newkirk was present with Greenlaw to hear the order; his remark, "Hope the RAF won't let them do all the work" (p. 90), becomes prophetic. More than two months later, after a great deal of air combat, Greenlaw would indicate that "at no time had the RAF in Burma ever co-operated with the AVG in giving us weather reports, arrivals and departures, or other vital information" (p. 126). Other memoirs corroborate this view. Sometimes the example is comic, as when crew chief Frank Losonsky mentions that "the British absolutely refused to let us boresight in late afternoon. The machine gun fire interfered with the peace and quiet of their 'tea time'" (p. 43). In *China: The Remembered Life,* Paul Frillmann faults the British for not having a warning network such as Chennault had perfected and asked them to devise one for Rangoon's defense, only to be told "that British spotters could not survive in the jungle, and the Burmese were not to be trusted" (p. 88). Much worse was the RAF practice of not sharing even the most vital information when they had it. Pappy Boyington is surprised to learn this when in *Baa Baa Black Sheep* he arrives at Mingaladon Field and is told the first alert of any enemy attack will not be a scramble order but the sight of two RAF Brewsters taking off "in a westerly direction, regardless of the wind sock. That's the signal" (p. 55). Wouldn't American pilots, with their own lives at risk and just as eager to gain the altitude needed to stand a chance against the Japanese, protest such thoughtlessness? If they did, it was to no avail, for as Olga Greenlaw tells it an AVG radioman had to loiter around the RAF control office, "jump up and answer [the phone] quickly before the British had a chance to get at it," hear the news and then seize the tannoy microphone, audible all over the field, and yell "Go get 'em, cowboys!" (pp. 126-27), a practice that worked only because the British controllers didn't understand the American's slang.

Not surprisingly, as the war continues, diary confidences turn nasty. "Had a sorry breakfast at the field mess and heard that the Japs are driving on Singapore," Charlie Bond writes on February 1. "Moulmein fell last night. The British cannot stem the tide, and I wonder if they are waiting for the Aussies or the Americans to do it for them" (p. 91). The ease British personnel took in performing their duties was particularly infuriating and gave larger appraisals such as Bond's a credibility well beyond any fairness. On a ferrying mission to Africa, where urgently needed P-40E Kittyhawks were waiting to be flown to the AVG in China, R.T. Smith found himself delayed in Egypt because of minor electrical problems, something the RAF could easily fix for him. They eventually did, but at their leisure. "The damned stupid British tied things up as usual" is how Smith tells it to his diary on March 7, 1942, adding, "I get sicker of them every day—no wonder the tea-drinking stoops get hell kicked out of them in every battle." In a footnote added to this page when his diary is published, Smith puts it in a more generous perspective:

> My, my, it seems I was in a bit of a snit at this point, perhaps with some justification. The RAF people often seemed determined to take their own sweet time about getting things done; their attitude was sometimes expressed by "what's the bloody 'urry, Yank?" In fairness it should be remembered that the war was new to us and with typical American impatience we wanted to win it in a hurry and go home. The British, of course, had been at it for over two years and seemed resigned to the fact that it would go on indefinitely. (p. 239)

Yet the ill feeling carries on throughout the trip, and even when things are going better and he's overnighting in Bahrain on the Persian Gulf, Smith chooses the Imperial Airways Hotel (and a hefty bill) to Royal Air Force accommodations: "Could have stayed at the RAF camp, but we're all getting so we can't speak to the damn Limeys with a civil tongue, so we're glad to get away from them" (p. 248).

Disgust with their British allies eventually became a staple of AVG mess hall comedy, as in the skit Olga Greenlaw recalls as devised for visiting guests, the question "What is the latest retreat the RAF has completed" being answered with "We haven't caught them yet to find out" (p. 167). When Singapore falls on February 15, the mood turns to serious depression. "Everyone is disgusted as hell the way things are going and at the inadequateness of the British in all respects," AVGer George Burgard is quoted in Duane Schultz's *The Maverick War*. "Rangoon is certainly much more of a soft touch than Singapore and here we sit, twenty-two AVG pilots trying to defend it against a nation. What prize chumps we are, holding down the hot spots for the British" (pp. 187-88). Even retreating together proves a disaster. At one field the RAF removes the sole radar set days before the AVG is ready to leave; at another, where the two forces try to cooperate, attempts to fuel up the departing convoy fail when the British forget where the gasoline is hidden. In the most preposterous scene of all, an RAF squadron lingers at Mingaladon and asks the AVG to help them dedicate their new officers' club the night before they're scheduled to burn it down for the evacuation. Finally, the AVG convoy that's been limping back to China pauses overnight at the British hill station in Maymyo, a colonial vacation spot maintained as impeccably as any countryside retreat in Surrey or Kent. Here Paul Frillmann is surprised to see everything as luxurious and peaceful as it ever was, including a posh social life: "I even saw two proper blondes in long-skirted evening dresses, one blue, one pink, walking sedately with two young British officers. Off to a dance, I supposed. They looked strange as Martians to me" (p. 122).

What had been left behind was ghastly in its devastation. Rangoon was a wasteland of burned buildings, looted shops, corpses decaying in the streets, and anyone remaining caught in a riotous struggle between native and colonial populations. Civil order had long since crumbled; rather than being left to starve, criminals, lunatics, lepers, and people otherwise critically ill were turned out of prisons and hospitals to fend for themselves; the scenes of them wandering through the blasted streets were nightmarish. When anyone did look back, it was to see a landscape seemingly floating in the dust. As historian Daniel Ford describes it in *Flying Tigers*, "The spectacular sunsets resulted from the dust and flame attending the collapse of the British Empire" (p. 252).

People of the American Volunteer Group were not sympathetic witnesses to this scene, either in its realistic or symbolic dimensions. Too much of their attitude had been spoiled by bad impressions beforehand, whether it be the red tape on the docks or the failure at even minimal cooperation at the airfields. In a novel that has no shortage of easy targets for its satire, Pappy Boyington's *Tonya* takes indecent fun with the British, such as when the AVG, hearing the first news of the Japanese strike at Pearl Harbor and the crippling of America's Pacific fleet, phones the British commander in Singapore to ask if they're under air attack as well. "Great heavens, no!" the Brigadier exclaims. "This is an impregnable naval base, my good fellow!" Well, is there anything at all out of the ordinary to report? "Let me think a moment," comes the reply, then "—oh, I say we had a corking good party at the Raffles Hotel last Saturday night!" (p. 141). The tragedy in Boyington's slapstick is that the call was really made, as was the reply quoted. Never to be outdone, even by the former lover who made her look so bad (along with everyone else) in *Tonya*, Olga Greenlaw packs her own book with ridiculous scenes about the British, hilarious in every way except that they're brutally true. Throughout *The Lady and the Tigers* she's drawn comic relief from a person named Stanley Robins, the individual who serves as her typically old-fashioned British colonial type. For much of the narrative he's off tiger hunting or drinking at his club. During the retreat from Burma it's in another club that they meet, with Stanley eager to prove at last how his skill bagging the great Bengal cats has not gone to waste. "The last two nights in Rangoon I spent shooting native looters," he boasts. "I was surprised at what a good shot I was, thought I'd lost the knack of it" (p. 243) But it's on the last leg of her escape that Greenlaw makes her serious point about the British, when during a breakdown she trades some catnapping RAF pilots a carton of cigarettes and a bottle of whisky for one of their spare Jeep tires:

> "All right," said the first officer, "go and get it and it's yours."
> "You are certainly taking it easy, aren't you?" I said to the first officer.
> "Oh, well," he answered, "we can't do anything about it. No

planes to fly, might as well get out of the way and move north." He laughed.

I said, "Why don't you get hold of a gun and do a little fighting?"

"What for?" he asked. "Something went wrong here. Maybe it is because we are not in the spirit of the thing. Now, back there in Dunkirk—that was different. There we were fighting for something. But here, who the hell cares for these Burmans?"

I thought to myself—so that's the attitude of these British soldiers toward the country they conquered. They take from it but give nothing in return. (p. 166)

Being a writer who has looked over the American Volunteer Group's Anglo-Burmese girlfriends and found them "a little too much on the dusky side" to suit her sense of decorum makes her the last person to be giving an anticolonialistic critique. Britain may have benefited economically from these people, but it had hardly enslaved them. And in England itself, a generation beyond the Empire's end, prejudices and discriminations lingered far less than in America nearly a century after emancipation. Just opposite the page in Russell Whelan's *The Flying Tigers* where the author had shown the AVG arrivals learning how American Lend-Lease supplies were blocked by British red tape, he marvels at the "sight of so many tanned and muscular young men with an identical gleam in their eyes," diverse as their backgrounds are: "a typical assortment of American names and racial strains" (p. 37), not even considering the fact that there are no African Americans in the unit (one of the strict USAAF principles that this otherwise unconventional group retained intact). Yet Greenlaw's stricture is not unfounded, for it was being made at the time and even earlier by major English writers such as George Orwell, whose novel *Burmese Days* (1934) uses the author's experience as a police officer in the region to underscore similar claims.

Well beyond such political issues is the culture clash Chennault's AVG men experienced in the Burma of 1941. The natives could be accepted as exotic, but the colonials from England—that was where the trouble lay. Caught unawares by the lulling security of a common language and so many shared traditions, American flyers were thrown off guard around the world, especially in England itself, where the Eagle Squadron members had to make unforeseen adjustments to warm beer, cold food, damp weather, early closing hours at the pubs, low pay, rationed goods, and, above all, the slower pace of British life. Thankfully one of the Eagles was Jim Goodson, familiar with British life thanks to family connections and prewar visits, who could advise his more naive squadron mates that "the secret of enjoying life in this country is never to be in a hurry," as he recalls in *Tumult in the Clouds* (1983). "If you push them, they resent it. It's kind of like an Old Folks Home" (p. 60). The Americans in the AVG did push hard, and as Erik Shilling notes in *Destiny*, "We could feel the resentment" (p. 118). Sometimes the provocation was passive, as going to the fleabag of a movie house in Toungoo not to view the film but, as Robert B. Hotz reports it, "to watch the British colonials arrive in formal evening dress and sit stiffly through a film while cockroaches scuttled across the floor and swooping bats threw shadows on the screen" (p. 118). Other times it was their own behavior, such as the night after their first air battle over Rangoon when much of the squadron descended on the plushly formal Silver Grill wearing dirty shirts, oily shorts, and mosquito boots, pistols slung on their hips, and Anglo-Burmese girlfriends (never allowed in the club) clinging to their arms, ready to teach the girls how to jitterbug while drinking each other under the tables. Such introductions did not bode well, and when working relationships were built on the Americans' belief that the British were waiting for the AVG to win the war for them only the worst could be expected.

Not surprisingly, AVG men hit if off much better with RAF personnel from elsewhere. Radioman Robert M. Smith hears from a ground crewman just back from the first battles in Rangoon that, although RAF officers showed little in their own combats, "the New Zealand pilots were wonderful, and some of the British sergeant pilots did all right on the second raid" (p. 50). The best explanation for such a claim may not be aerial records but, as historian Daniel Ford reports, the fact that these New Zealanders were happy to play cards with their AVG buddies (p. 242). R.T. Smith's praise is similarly centered on how things seemed on the ground, agreeing that when it came to pilots from New Zealand and Australia "we hit it off much better with them than with the more reserved Britishers who often seemed quite snobbish" (p. 156). It will be remembered that on Smith's ferrying trip across the Middle East he had to avoid spending time with RAF people, so dilatory had their attitudes been toward getting him and his new P-40E back to China on schedule. On a similar trip Erik Shilling stops in Cairo and has an entirely different type of experience, thanks to the special folks he meets:

> A couple of us were drinking at a bar one night and met several friendly Aussies, fighter pilots from a group based in the North African desert. They were in Cairo on a two week R and R [rest and recreation leave], and incidentally, were from the same group flying the shark nosed P-40 we'd seen in the papers. Their sense of humor was similar to Americans', so we got along famously and soon became friends. We palled around with them until their leave was over, and with their help we were introduced to many desirable bars, and also some that weren't. (p. 160)

Apart from the stuffier civilians' shock at the AVG's seemingly uncouth behavior, British views of their new American allies were much more generous than the way Chennault's people thought of them. But from the very top there was a difference in both strategy and tactics that made close cooperation a fatuous hope. General Archibald Wavell, commanding the entire region from India, greeted America's entrance into the war by expecting the AVG to be assimilated into the RAF, from his point of view the only established air arm in the area. Chennault, of course, succeeded in resisting this. But when the two air forces took off to engage Japanese adversaries, differences became more painfully obvious. Having studied the enemy since 1937, Chennault had learned that the only way to beat their vastly more maneuverable aircraft was to swoop down on them for a quick strike and then zoom away. These literal hit-and-run tactics, which to this point were more characteristic of hot-rodders and gangsters than to the knighthood of the air, were complemented by two-plane formations that also went against the book. For the prewar RAF, there had been an actual manual consisting of attacking styles numbered in ascending sequence and involving a full squadron of twelve fighters forming various ranks to approach the enemy in orderly fashion; once engaged, the planes could then be expected to conduct themselves by classic *mano a mano* rules of the dogfight. For Chennault, such practice was a formula for disaster. Instead, he taught his volunteers to think in terms of two-plane units for all stages of the fight—before, during, and after—and to visualize what those two planes did as the work of a boxer's pair of hands, one covering while the other landed its punch.

Needless to say, tactics of the gangster and the boxer did not appeal to the still inexperienced RAF commanders in the Far East. As Chennault mentions in his *Way of a Fighter*, "At Rangoon the RAF 221st Group posted a notice that any RAF pilot seen diving away from a fight would be subject to court-martial" (p. 114). On this same page, he contrasts the results, RAF pilots barely breaking even against the Japanese "while the Americans rolled up a 15 to 1 score." Granted, British flyers were trained in methods that had worked against the heavier German and Italian aircraft, but "against the acrobatic Japs" the results were suicidal.

"Our losses were higher than they should have been because the advice from the American Volunteer Group had not been properly learned"—these words come from M.C. "Bush" Cotton's *Hurricanes over Burma* (1995) and reflect the educational experience British pilots underwent during the first months of 1942, when the AVG's war in the Far East became their own as well. Cotton, whose service nickname reflected his Australian nationality, had left home to train in Canada and begin operations in England, soon after which he shipped out from Scotland for the Middle East. Leaving on December 5, 1941, his destination was Basra on the Persian Gulf, where he and his colleagues were to pick up their Hurricanes and fly on to the Caucasus, where they expected to help the Russian Army by destroying Panzer tanks. All that changed with the news of Pearl Harbor, a change the quickness of which amazed the young flyer:

> In retrospect, one can imagine the difficulties involved in the reassessment of priorities of the whole field of battle that the Allied war planners now had to make. It says a lot for the speed with which they acted, for, within a few days of the U.S. involvement, the Durban Castle was diverted to berth at Freetown in Sierra Leone. Half of the pilots of the three squadrons were off-loaded, and the remainder rejoined the convoy to proceed to Singapore as reinforcements for the squadrons there and, as it turned out, virtual oblivion. One of these pilots was John Gorton of 135 Squadron, who survived Singapore to become a prime minister of Australia. (p. 118)

Bush Cotton was one of those to leave the ship at Freetown, from whence DC-2 transports of the RAF flew him and his squadron mates to Khartoum. Here he met Barry Sutton, flight commander in another squadron on its way to the Far East, who would himself write a narrative starting with this journey, *Jungle Pilot* (1946), a sequel to the already famous account of his 1940 exploits flying in the Battle of France and the Battle of Britain, *The Way of a Pilot* (1942). These two pilots continued East until they reached Burma, but en route to Singapore was another Battle of Britain veteran and already published author, Arthur Gerald Donahue. Art Donahue was an American flying with the RAF since the summer of 1940, well in advance of his country's other volunteers who would become the Eagle Squadrons, and had written *Tally Ho! Yankee in a Spitfire* (1941). From his Far East experience Donahue would write another book, *Last Flight from Singapore* (1943). Donahue's contingent had left earlier than Cotton's, the ground crews embarking from Liverpool on November 11, 1941, and most of the pilots following at month's end. Among them was not just Donahue but a third author, Terence Kelly, who would in later years publish three books on his years in the Far East with the RAF. Like Donahue, he thought the desert equipment they carried meant their fighting would take place in Libya; after Pearl Harbor their convoy was reorganized in Durban with Singapore as its new goal. Of these early reinforcements, only two subsequent authors knew from the start where they were being sent: Kenneth Hemingway, who as a prewar journalist had already published a book on industrial conditions and would soon write *Wings over Burma* (1944), and Terence O'Brien, who much later would author three volumes covering his participation in all aspects of the war from Singapore's fall to its recapture in 1945. Hemingway left soon after December 7, convoying to Africa and then flying a Hurricane as escort to five Blenheims destined for Rangoon. O'Brien flew all the way, taking a flight of Hudson bombers the distance to Singapore, leaving England December 29, by which point the nature of this new war with the Japanese was all too clear.

Because his travels would take him to Singapore, Sumatra, and Java before returning to a posting in England via India and Ceylon, Art Donahue never met the American Volunteer Group. Nor does he mention their existence. It is unlikely, however, that he would have been their notable advocate, for even the much better disciplined and exceptionally more regular Eagle Squadrons had not won any enthusiasm from this earlier arrival, who'd learned everything within the Royal Air Force and preferred it that way, talking his way out of assignment to the Eagles when they became operational. His *Last Flight to Singapore* does take a unique angle on America's entry into the war, for Donahue learns about it in the midst of his trip East, where in the East he doesn't know but hopefully some place where the action is as hot as it was during the Battle of Britain.

"I felt dazed and overwhelmed," Donahue recalls, having been told the news of Japan's sneak attack. "After all the fighting that we Americans in the RAF had been through, believing that we were helping to make this unnecessary, it had come at last, all in a twinkling, and our country was committed to take part in the slaughter" (p. 18). His response is much different from that of Chennault's volunteers just finishing their training in Burma. The record of their own reactions speaks for vindication of foresight and eagerness to make war against the Japanese with their country's might behind them. Donahue, as should be expected from his unwillingness to join the Eagles, responds less as someone who has been flying for adventure than as a fighter pilot who volunteered for Britain as a way of keeping America out of the war rather than bringing his country into the fray. As his convoy ship rests in Gibraltar, its destination even now being reconsidered, Donahue joins his colleagues in worrying for what this newly restructured future bodes for them: "Everyone was subdued—we Americans because of the tragedy it spelled for our country, and the others because we felt it would lengthen the war to have Japan added to our enemies. The only bright side for us Americans was knowing that we wouldn't be outlaws any more in the eyes of our own country—as we were when I went home on leave to the States the previous winter and wasn't allowed to wear my uniform" (p. 18).

As the other reinforcing pilots head to the Far East, their thoughts are like those of American Volunteer Group recruits, anticipating the experience in literary terms—Kipling's poems and stories, the *Rubáiyát* verses of Edward FitzGerald, and, as Barry Sutton admits in *Jungle Pilot,* "the India which is the happy hunting-ground of the Romanesque novelist to whom this country and its way of life is a melody on a theme of breath-taking landscape, chukkas and chotah pegs, houseboats and cocktails, gracious and cultivated rajahs; a lyric India, admitting of no more than the echo of discords such as disease, hate, and poverty; a microcosmic India, as unreal and precious and remote as a snow scene within a glass bowl" (p. 120). Although the literary references are made early in Sutton's memoir, the comments on India come from its conclusion, when he realizes how privileged he has been to see these last views of a subcontinent already swept by nationalist fervor and soon to go its own way from that of the British Empire. In the full set of literary allusions can be found a major difference between an AVG and RAF citation of the same bookish source: for Americans, these writings are aesthetic materials, matters for lyric art, belletristic in the sharpest sense of that word, whereas for the English, Kipling and FitzGerald and their like are readable not only as the record of colonialism but as a testament whose fidelty to fact is fast fading (if not having been erased altogether). Yet even along the way exotic sights and sounds distract these pilots from the military reality awaiting them. Sutton himself feasts on the sights and sounds of Africa, the Middle East, and India. But he is also mindful of the different quality of human life, especially at airfields swarming with low-caste workers vulnerable to being run over like ants—for the balance of his trip the author keeps telling himself that the thud he heard on takeoff could not have been his Hurricane's wing striking and killing one of these unfortunates.

What the incoming RAF pilots saw among their compatriots was as disconcerting as any scene witnessed by the AVG. Not even in the Middle East, where attention was fixed on the Germans and Italians, was there much awareness of danger from the Japanese. Wing Commander Cedric A.C. "Bunny" Stone was another flyer diverted en route after Pearl Harbor. His memoirs are reproduced as part of Bush Cotton's *Hurricanes over Burma*, and early on Stone complains that "the Middle East HQ were not interested in the rapidly Rising Sun casting its shadows in the Far East." As he and his men make the customary stopover in Cairo, he's shocked to hear what would become the customary expression that "'Oh, the Japs; they cannot fly and are blind anyway—they all wear glasses!'—comforting at the time, but how mistaken!" (p. 230). Closer to the action in Burma and even after the Japanese air offensive against Rangoon has begun, Kenneth Hemingway marvels at the atmosphere that characterizes India in the early months of 1942:

There had been a peace-time air about Karachi, Jodhpur, Allahabad, Calcutta, like the feeling aboard a ship in a convoy when you pace the deck and think of your wife at home, or one of the quiet Hertfordshire villages you knew, comparatively untouched by raiders. In Calcutta, at the open-air restaurant, I had sat out listening to a good band, drinking as much as I pleased, watching the crowd happy and gay as any in pre-war England or France. If the possibility of being bombed was discussed at all, it was a contingency remote as a raid from Mars. It was not the people's fault. Although, a year later, they were to crouch down as London had crouched, listening for the

> drone of radials, at the time when we were in Rangoon the war
> had been kept out of India by the Afghanistan ranges, the
> Tibetan plateau, and the jungle hills of Burma and Malay. They
> were like inhabitants of a house on a hummock who still
> played cards behind curtained windows, ignorant of the flood-
> water rising up their garden path. And I remembered my wife
> saving an egg for me when I went home on leave in England—the
> menu at the Grand had about twenty items. For breakfast I could
> have had two, three, four omelettes, if I had wished. (p. 27)

As the egg episode shows, English flyers could be even
more shocked by the unapparency of war out here; unlike
the AVG recruits, who'd left a country at peace, these RAF
flyers were coming from a country fighting for its life against
an enemy still with the odds in its favor. In *Hurricanes over
Burma*, Bush Cotton, notwithstanding his Australian nationality and Canadian training, is likewise "staggered by the
peacetime attitudes of the military services in India, particularly at Karachi, with life being lived as though nothing had
happened since 1939." Servants at hand, visiting cards re-
quired for dropping by clubs and the homes of senior officers, dances conducted with all the protocol of royalty being
present—to Cotton and his colleagues bound for a very real
shooting war in Burma these practices seemed preposterous, "so we tried to break down some of this wasteful and
tiresome rubbish by being as anti-establishment as we could
get away with" (p. 121), to the extent of taking over the
orchestra's instruments for a jazz jam session and teaching
the locals how to jitterbug. After flying and fighting in
Burma, Cotton is all the more adamant. "It never failed to
make me mad as hell to meet up with some of the asinine
English fatheads who seemed to congregate in India," he
confides. "Perhaps the Brits got rid of them out of their island, to India, in the same way as they used to send their
convicts to Australia" (p. 150), a sentiment more than one
AVGer might share. Even much later on, when formally stationed in Calcutta and operating his squadron off a street in
a suddenly threatened downtown, this outspoken memoirist enjoys recounting how he and his friends bought
monocles and wore them to the officers' club, "Putting on

the most frightful Pommy accents . . . and talking loud drivel" until the resident Colonel Blimps threw them out of the place. Bunny Stone puts it in perspective, observing how "the whole Far East at that time" maintained an insufferable laissez-aller attitude "until the arrival of Lord Louis Mountbatten and General Orde Wingate in 1943," whose presence finally answered the commonly voiced question of "How did Britain ever win a war?" (p. 231).

Rear area complacency extended to Burma as well. Although by the time these reinforcements arrived, Rangoon was in the thick of it and could not provide scenes of colonial ease and indolence that had shocked the AVG, hill-station retreats such as Maymyo, positioned well above Mandalay, maintained a sense of peacefulness even as the capital burned and the whole country prepared to fall. Kenneth Hemingway earned a rest period here after several weeks of combat; because it was an official Army cantonment, he expected rows of barracks and bare parade grounds. Instead, he found Maymyo looking like a combination prewar English resort and Middlesex suburb where everyone acted in proper style—a style that had once been expensive and now was fully unobtainable at home, but which could be purchased here for the paltriest of sums.

Trained as a journalist, Hemingway knows how to find the right descriptive subject for the point he wants to make. And so after quickly detailing the grass verges bordering the well-built English homes and noting how even the local waiters are acting just like their counterparts at Blackpool and in the Lake Country, he sits back at dinner to observe what is to him the most telling scene: how the British women living at this station behave.

There were quite a number of them, he counts, appreciating how they are mostly young, recently married or engaged to officers or civilian careerists, each group having chosen colonial postings for the obvious benefits of lifestyle, earnings, and advancement. The men might well be facing danger in these newly warlike times, but as for the women— "My impression, and it holds to this day, was that they were conscious of being women, and white!" Hemingway's frankness is redoubled when he gives the reason why, because "their bodies were—and are—at a premium in tropical countries." With servants, housework is not their worry. Nor is any type of work at all. Instead, "they have all day to make themselves sleek by exercise, good food, a nap in the afternoon—as a result of which they tend to fatten in the rump earlier than women at home." The author doesn't blame them for taking such an easy road, but nevertheless feels "that there is something fundamentally amiss." None of them, he fears, "appreciate[s] the privilege of living as they do in a stimulating, interesting foreign country." Instead, "their brains become bemused by slavish male attention, gin, and 'Oh, ayah, don't forget to put John to bed early,' or, 'Tennis, darling, of course, just a set; then we'll have some of those lovely cream cakes at Straboli's, eh!'" (p. 136).

Further east, in Singapore, Art Donahue would see much of the same, and in an outpost even more direly threatened. When it does fall and he gets out in a literal version of his book's title, *Last Flight from Singapore*, he feels compelled to review what he has seen of these peacetime conditions maintained throughout the coming of war and even to the moment of defeat. "I reflected that in two and a half months these new enemies had overrun Malaya, Singapore, and Sumatra in rapid succession. They were winning in the Philippines and other places, and I thought to myself, 'Where are we going to stop them?'" But another thought soon follows, one that makes him shiver: "*Are* we going to stop them?" Ultimacies pile up faster than Donahue can handle, while his thoughts turn back to first causes:

> Was it possible that we were really losing this war? Were these perhaps the last days of our civilization?
> Surely I had seen out here most of the things that had preceded the fall of other great civilizations—the softness and decadence that come from easy living—the lack of appreciation for the good things of life that comes from the too easy attainment of them—the failure to appreciate freedom that comes from taking it for granted too long. (p. 153)

Yet it is just one theater, only a weakly garrisoned outpost being overwhelmed by the full strength of a great nation near at hand. Above all, Donahue can see that colonial ease is an entirely different issue from what is really at stake in World War II:

> I, if anyone, should certainly know that the "things that were bad" out here were not typically British, for I had served more than a year in England, where the universal fighting spirit and loyalty had made me feel very inferior. The people there were anything but decadent, and the miserable creatures who had let down their King and country so woefully out here were no more true British than the fifth columnists and saboteurs in my own country were true Americans. (p. 154)

Despite the pride shown in England's determination during the Battle of Britain and the Blitz, Donahue's words carry a sentiment that is more American than British. Unwilling to feel much sympathy for the far reaches of empire, he neglects the fact that some of his RAF colleagues could trace family histories (and in some cases family fortunes) to these colonies. Together with Canadians, Australians, and New Zealanders, there were pilots from Rhodesia and South Africa flying in these units, not to mention the massive contribution made by the Empire Training Scheme. Without these resources England could never have held out, let alone eventually won the war, and one of its war aims was to maintain the colonies. John Slessor, who during the war held many top command and staff positions, writes in *The Central Blue* (1956) that his American allies never seemed to understand that there were postwar considerations that shaped Britain's role during hostilities. "You old Limeys are always thinking about the Middle East and the route to India and all that sort of thing *after* the war," he describes an American friend complaining. "Our job is to beat the Germans and win the war and to hell with anything else," went the argument that would have none of Slessor's question of "what we wanted to win the war *for*, if it was not to create the situation we wanted to see *after* the war" (p. 345). What Britain envisioned for the postwar world was not in line with American aims. Geopolitically, the United States considered China an important force, and insisted on building a Far East strategy around Chiang's armies and governments, neither of which interested the British (who rather than consolidating strengths north of Burma wished to drive on to recapture Rangoon, preferably with amphibious landings, and then continue on to Singapore and the Dutch East Indies). While American plans centered on blocking Japan's western flank by strengthening China and moving for a knockout blow across the Pacific from the east, Churchill lobbied for colonial reestablishment, in a minute quoted by Henry Probert in *The Forgotten Air Force* (1995). "The political importance of our making some effort to recover British territory must not be underrated," the Prime Minister emphasizes. "Rangoon and Singapore are great names in the British eastern world, and it will be an ill-day for Britain if the war ends without our having made a stroke to regain these places and having let the whole Malay peninsula alone until it is eventually evacuated as the result of an American-dictated peace at Tokyo" (pp. 217-18). From the moment in 1942 when the first attempts to reoccupy Burma began, the two Allies were at cross-purposes: the Americans under Stilwell marching in, as they had marched out, covering the territory foot by foot while strengthening supply lines to China along the way, as opposed to British desires for quicker aerial and amphibious assaults with an eye to taking back the major commercial centers. None of this, however, was as hostile as British and American relations over clandestine operations in Indo-China. Terence O'Brien's *The Moonlight War* (1987) tells of the subterfuges he and his colleagues had to practice in order to aid the French, whom the United States didn't want assisted because of their Vichy association and their country's postwar intent to maintain the region as a colony; Probert's *The Forgotten Air Force* suggests that at one point American fighters may have shot down RAF planes involved in such work (pp. 211-12).

None of these geopolitical concerns was on the minds of the RAF reinforcements when, in January and February of 1942, they met their AVG counterparts who, together with the obsolete Brewster Buffalo squadrons, had been fighting the Japanese over Rangoon since late December. Granted, in their early planning the Royal Air Force leadership had tried to co-opt the AVG to the purposes of empire. In *The Central Blue,* John Slessor tells of T.V. Soong approaching him and Lord Lothian during staff conferences in Washington, D.C., to join in the organizational efforts, supplying veteran pilots as squadron or flight commanders and sending over some senior command and staff personnel. Although logistics eventually made such cooperation impossible, Slessor had nevertheless recommended it, knowing that if British installations in the Far East were attacked they'd be on their own, whereas being a part of the AVG would "prove a useful investment" (p. 337). Now, almost exactly a year later, the American Volunteer Group was more American than ever, as memoirists such as Kenneth Hemingway, Bush Cotton, and Barry Sutton were to record.

"We stood there and frankly eyed one another," the author of *Wings over Burma* recalls of a mess hall encounter with the AVG, "like members of friendly bandit gangs meeting" (p. 121). By this time the Hurricane pilot had learned enough about Chennault's men to know they were good company for a pint and a natter, but his first look at them was rather disconcerting. Arriving at Mingaladon airfield to take up his duties in the defense of Rangoon, Hemingway is just being told about such essentials as Army positions and the warning system when, as he notes, "My attention was diverted to a newcomer, a well-built fellow of medium height, dressed in shirt and trousers and having a revolver slung in an unorthodox, finely-worked leather holster." Tired and dusty, the man looks dangerous, but when he asks the squadron commander "Got'ny beer, Stone?" Hemingway realizes that "here was one of the AVG—the 'Flying Tigers' whose pseudonym was no overstatement" (p. 18). The American is Bob Neale, and he and the new RAF pilot get along fine. Afterward Squadron Leader Bunny Stone assures him that fears about "that tough gallimaufry of mercenaries" are needless—that both the AVG and the RAF had their reputations to maintain, but that "thank heaven we had the sense to sit down quietly and listen to them, when we first arrived" (p. 19).

Bunny Stone's own narrative, appearing at the end of

Bush Cotton's *Hurricanes over Burma,* confirms that one of the first things this squadron leader did was seek knowledge from the AVG. Not that first impressions were any easier for him than they were for Kenneth Hemingway. One easily pictures Stone, ramrod straight and properly mannered as any English commanding officer should be, entering the American quarters and asking "one of the reclining forms, cigar in mouth and Coke bottle in hand (which made me feel that I had strayed onto the set of a Western), if I could see the commanding officer" (p. 236). Lazily motioned over toward Jack Newkirk, Stone is pleased to learn that the AVG squadron leader is "polite, which was unusual because, at that time, the British and Americans did not altogether see eye to eye" (p. 237). Although Stone never got the AVG's command structure straight—his memoir accords Chennault's staff officer Harvey Greenlaw a general's rank, the nickname "Pappy," and further confuses him with CAMCO director William Pawley—he does listen closely to Newkirk and learns the proper hit-and-run method for dealing with the Japanese, "a reversal of our tactics in Britain with the Hurricane and the Messerschmitt 109s, which we could out-turn and shoot down if they stayed with us" (p. 238). What helps most, however, is that Stone has two Americans in his RAF squadron, Tex Barrick and Ken Wisrodt, who spend much time in the AVG mess among their countrymen who had previously been keeping to themselves.

Kenneth Hemingway himself hits it off well with the AVG. Early passages find him doting on their Wild West accents, while before long he's adopting their mannerisms, he and a colleague visiting Rangoon with "both of us swinging a gun at our hips like a couple of cowboys come to town" (p. 60) and later counseling a style of vehicle dispersal at their airfield "as the pioneers in America could have prepared for a Red Indian attack" (p. 61). Even at the end, during the retreat from Burma that brought renewed friction to British-American relationships, he can remark that "the boys had been enthusiastic at the prospect of carrying on with the AVG" from bases in the north and regret that "it could not be, no machines could be spared from the defence of

India" (p. 188). Why the better RAF pilots liked flying alongside the American volunteers is evident from Barry Sutton's
enthusiasm for this unit's élan—not just for their Wild West
manners, as so impressed Kenneth Hemingway, but for the
fighting spirit they brought to the two squadrons' joint operations. Sutton sees it one morning at Mingaladon when
the air raid siren sounds and the Flying Tigers scramble from
their line across the field. "Through the trees I could see dust
rising from the AVG dispersal and hear the staccato swear-
ing of the Allison engines of the Tomahawks as they taxied
out to the strip before taking off," he says in a central passage from *Jungle Pilot*. "They had an air of aggression, these
Tomahawks, I remember thinking, and it was prompted by
something less obvious than the long, vicious nose painted
as a tiger. Their engines always sounded angry, and as they
took off they curled back their wheels into their bellies as
though writhing in fury." What a contrast to the machine
Sutton flies, the Hawker Hurricane powered so smoothly
by its Rolls-Royce engine that in Battle of Britain accounts
was often said to sigh rather than roar and designed so beautifully by Sidney Camm that even its landing gear could disappear into its thin dihedral wings. "When four sections had
taken off," Sutton compares, "there came the familiar
smoother 'whoo-*oom*' of Hurricanes and three charged down
another runway from the direction of our own dispersal
point" (p. 52). Like the AVG pilots themselves, their equipment was rougher and meaner, mass produced in factory
assembly lines rather than hand built on benches by masters who in peacetime worked on the finest luxury automo-
biles. And the fighting style was more brutal, just the warning
Sutton and the other newly arrived pilots needed in this radically different theater of war.

How brutal the contrast could be is evident from Bunny
Stone's memoir, where he is less taken by the aggressive
aesthetics of the AVG than by the vicious way they treat their
adversary, part of a story that begins innocuously enough
with thoughts about finely made parachutes:

> The Japanese were equipped with beautiful silk para-

chutes—much in demand at home—but they seldom used them. I only witnessed one occasion. We were watching a fighter battle overhead, and a Japanese fighter pilot took to the silk about 2 miles away. I sent our medical officer over in a jeep. He was greeted by some of the American Volunteer Group just putting their smoking Colts back in their holsters. One of them drawled, "Guess you're too late, Doc. Reckon he's dead." He was indeed, with about twenty revolver bullets in him. This may sound barbarous now, but the American Volunteer Group were shot on sight if captured, and we had little time for the Japanese as a race because of their frightening barbarity towards the vanquished. Apart from the strangeness of the country, we were fighting with this added fear of capture. (p. 251)

The fight for Burma brackets what British strategists considered the more important concern for Singapore, which fell in mid-February of 1942, six weeks after Rangoon was first bombed but three weeks before the Burmese capital was evacuated. Air defense, particularly the mutual reinforcing operations of the RAF and AVG, made the difference. In *The Forgotten Air Force*, Henry Probert marvels at what "a narrow margin" prevailed in holding Rangoon so much longer. "On 27 February the combined fighter strength of the RAF and AVG was down to ten," yet even this small number allowed Rangoon to be left in a more orderly fashion than would have been obtained had the Japanese been allowed to interfere from the air, making the results more like Dunkirk (p. 89). Singapore was an entirely different matter, where the RAF was at all times catastrophically outnumbered and could expect little help from Britain and none at all from the AVG. Terence O'Brien's flight of Hudson bombers was, in fact, delayed at Toungoo, where he pulled up alongside a line of AVG planes for refueling only to be detained by a RAF commander who felt he should be staying there to help hold Burma. "Not again, for Christ's sake!" he cries, one of the many frustrations noted in his *Chasing After Danger* (1990, p. 174), as obstacle after obstacle retards his progress to Singapore. O'Brien's delay was just the most recent of many disappointments for what England considered its premier outpost in the Far East, a position so important to its global role that John Slessor, when taking part in the American-British-Canadian Staff Conversations of February and March 1941, urged his counterparts in Washington, D.C., that "instead of keeping the [U.S.] Pacific Fleet concentrated at Honolulu, thousands of miles from anywhere, they should send a powerful force to be based on Singapore" (*The Central Blue*, pp. 346-47). That didn't happen; but neither did Slessor and his planning staff foresee how Singapore would fall, not to a superior naval force but to air attack and a land advance down the Malay Peninsula, which had been considered just as impassable as the Ardennes Forest before Germany's surprise thrust in May 1940 (p. 229).

"Everything hung on Singapore," Art Donahue could appreciate as he convoyed east in *Last Flight from Singapore*. "If it fell, the enemy would be able to conquer the Dutch East Indies, which would give them rubber, tin, and oil that they needed to continue the war" (p. 21). Indeed, the British had known this since 1921, when the collapse of previous naval agreements with the Japanese had dictated the need for greater Royal Navy presence in the area, a region that in the early 1930s was made part of Japan's designs for an "East Asian Co-Prosperity Sphere" as a way of becoming a world power itself. For the Western world, however, these were decades of peace, a time scheme recognized by the British government's planning according to the "Ten Year Rule" that no war could be anticipated until at least that far in the future. When Donanhue's reinforcing unit arrived at the end of January, Sinagpore had been harried by air bombardments and enemy land forces had advanced to the straits separating the city from the peninsula already in Japanese hands. During the night he could hear the connecting causeway being demolished, and the next morning, January 31, 1942, "a BBC news broadcast began with the words, 'The Battle of Malaya has ended and the Battle for Singapore has begun!' We had arrived just in time to take part in the defense of an island under seige" (p. 32).

"It was easy to imagine RAF Station Tengah before the rot set in," Terence O'Brien recalls in *Chasing After Danger*, "—a month before we arrived say,—back at the beginning of December 1941 and still in local peace." As one of the fields defending Singapore, it had boasted an officers' mess terraced above lush green grass with a vista stretching out over a picturesquely cultivated rubber plantation and fading into the "misty blue hills" of the mainland to the north, from which the Japanese would soon come. "You could picture officers and guests out there on mess nights chatting under the Southern Cross, resplendent bearers in blue and gold livery carrying silver trays of drinks, behind them the strains of a waltz coming from the dance band in the spacious lounge brilliantly lit and aswirl in colour" (p. 179). Coming all the way by air with his flight of Hudson bombers, O'Brien was among the earliest reinforcements; yet even as the new year began, windows were shattered, doors were knocked loose, electricity and water and drainage had all failed, and the servants were long gone, all of it reminding the author of a doggerel about discovering a lighthouse abandoned in a disaster.

Devastation wrought by the first Japanese air attacks had taken its toll in personnel as well, less in terms of physical casualties than in spirit. In *The Forgotten Air Force,* Probert describes a large military staff (numbering 116 officers) rigidly adhering to time-wasting procedures of peacetime administration, as if routine order in their own offices would abate the chaos outside:

> Others echo the theme. A medical orderly at Selatar [the chief defensive airfield] compares those who arrived in Singapore in 1941 having been blooded in the United Kingdom with the "fat cats" who had been there longer, many of whom went to pieces after the shock of the first bombing. An LAC [leading aircraftsman, the top ground crew rank] in the marine section was struck when he arrived by the complacency and inexperience of the long-term residents; having been on the south coast of England during the Battle of Britain he was threatened with disciplinary action on one occasion for remaining at work after the sirens had sounded. An officer on 62 Squadron writes of the life of fair luxury and ease at Tengah in 1939/40 and the failure of the CO or squadron commanders to bring home the dangers facing them: only in October 1941 when an intelligence officer visited them at Alor Star [airfield]

did they become aware of the Japanese threat. An electrician
with the same squadron describes the conditions at Alor Star in
1941 as "definitely peacetime Air Force"—they were given no
training at all under wartime conditions. (p. 24)

Innocent of wartime realities to begin with, the established
Singapore forces were left that way, never given liasion visits
from the Air Ministry at home and rarely kept up to date with
news of recent operations and developments in tactics—hence
the surprise of flyers such as Art Donahue and Terence
O'Brien, who arrived fresh from an England at war to find
Singapore clinging so ludicrously to the trappings of peace.

There were more immediate command problems as well.
Though Japanese bombing raids were regular and predictable, basic precautions such as removing aircraft from the
theatened bases were not taken. "It was hard to contain the
anger and frustration felt at the stupidity of such a decision,"
Terence O'Brien explains, furious that his Hudsons brought
so dearly and desperately all the way from England were to
be left in the open as such easy and inevitable targets. "You
longed to trace it back, track it carefully through the corri-
dors of command until at last you found the fool who origi-
nated it, then kick him literally out of his office." If this
sounds revolutionary, the author agrees, recalling how "we
were not far from revolt that night," a group of the newly
arrived pilots conducting "a mutinous session" characterized by heavy drinking, loud criticism "of the calamitous
order," and damnations of those in control, none of whom
"made any attempt to quell the protest" (p. 184). Yet neither
did any of these staff officers make even the slightest attempt
to explain their reasoning, "an indication of the quality of
command in the Far East. It also explains why in that first
week the feeling among aircrews in the squadron varied
between mutinous fury and black despair" (p. 185).

From this initial low level, morale would only drop further as conditions worsened and odds grew hopelessly
longer. One line of study, the most obvious, suggests that
apart from any strengths of spirit and brilliance of command
the simple numbers were never there for even a chance at

holding off the Japanese, much less repelling them. Prewar planning had determined that 336 aircraft would be needed to defend Singapore adequately. Yet by the time European hostilities with Germany began, there were only twenty-four Blenheim medium bombers, ten flying boats (six of them obsolete), and twenty-four obsolescent biplane torpedo bombers on hand, with no fighters at all, meaning that while a naval assault might be at least minimally harried, there was no defense whatsoever against attack from the air. In view of this threat, four fighter squadrons were assigned to Singapore between February and October of 1941. Unfortunately, they were equipped only with what an embattled Britain could spare, which was the inferior Brewster Buffalo that had been tested and rejected by the RAF's Eagle Squadrons. When the Japanese attack came, there were just sixty-seven of them ready to fly. Counting everything, the RAF at Singapore could muster 181 aircraft, or scarcely more than half of what plans called for as the minimum—plans that anticipated neither land nor air assault.

Calendar dates in Japan's offensive turned quickly. On December 8, 1941, the international dateline allowed the first aerial bombardment of Singapore to coincide with the Pearl Harbor attack. On December 10, the Royal Navy's *Prince of Wales* and *Repulse* were sunk, in part because of ineffective use of air defense but mostly because their presence had been to act as a deterrence with no thought to what would happen if Japan were not deterred. By mid-December the Japanese Army had made key breakthroughs in its advance down the Malay Peninsula. By Christmastime, when aerial attacks on Rangoon began as well, Singapore had suffered repeated bombardments and on New Year's Day was anxiously awaiting help. By January 3, 1942, Terence O'Brien's flight of Hudson bombers and the first reinforcing convoy had arrived, followed on January 13 by a second convoy carrying fifty-one Hurricane fighters (supplemented between January 27 and 30 by forty-eight more flown off the aircraft carrier HMS *Indomitable*). But by then, as Art Donahue noted on arrival, the Japanese had chased the British off the mainland and were facing them across the straits separating Singapore Island from Johore.

On February 15, Singapore surrendered, a surprise to no one except the pilots who defended this key outpost. Although all the memoirists are in agreement that their talents could have been used more effectively, the most vehement in assigning blame is Terence Kelly, a Hurricane pilot in the *Indomitable* group who fought on through Sumatra. As he argues in *Hurricane and Spitfire Pilots at War* (1986), "Singapore fell not because the water supply was taken by the Japanese nor because the guns pointed in the wrong directions, but because by the time the outnumbered and lightly equipped Japanese had reached the north bank of the Johore Baru Strait the morale of the Allied troops was utterly broken." Why had morale collapsed so far in advance of actual surrender? A major factor was "the Japanese air superiority," which well beyond the relatively light tonnage of bombs dropped convinced the troops that they were defeated even before a final engagement could begin. After all, "the sight of apparently unresisted groups of bombers in Hendon Air Display formations arriving punctually every morning is distressing for an army which has known nothing but retreat for weeks and has believed, indeed been encouraged to believe, that once it has withdrawn to an island fortress all will be well" (p. 104).

Such evident Japanese air superiority need not have been, or at least the pilots claim. Because of the commanders' unfounded belief that Japanese Zeroes and Hayabusas could outfight Hurricanes, never were more than fourteen of the hundred or so available to the RAF sent up at a time. Yet, because there had been no thought given to intelligence work, Kelly and his colleagues took off from the *Indomitable* expecting "to clear the Jap wooden biplanes from the skies" (p. 106). When more formidable contemporary opponents were discovered, information was not collected and analyzed as had been done in the European theater. Comparisons of pilots' accounts could have determined just how well or how poorly Hurricanes and Spitfires matched up against newer Japanese fighters. In the rush to get men and planes to the

Far East, diverting them en route to other destinations, no squadron intelligence officers had been provided. Individual pilots surely knew how their planes performed against this newly encountered enemy, but there was no way to pool their information and organize successful strategies. Instead, the unexpected appearance of high-performance mono-planes was taken in official quarters as one more piece of alarmingly bad news to be added to the overall collapse of morale; by assuming that the Hurricane was no match for the Zero and its cousins, defeat was all the easier to accept and explain.

Bloody Shambles—the title of the two-volume study (1992 and 1993) by Christopher Shores and Brian Cull with Yasuho Ozawa—aptly characterizes how things went for the British in the Far East, and in Singapore especially. Command problems reached all the way down to the municipal engineers responsible for digging air raid trenches. One said dig them straight, and they were; then another official from the government said no, dig them zig zagged, and that was redone; finally, a third official insisted that the trenches should be refilled, lest mosquitos be encouraged to breed. "A compromise was reached," the authors report, "and the trenches, which were only three feet deep to start with, were subsequently half-filled!" (1:150). More seriously, an inability to agree on labor rates prevented the construction of north coast defenses for the island until it was too late, the local council's excuse being that such payments would promote economic inflation. The authors' quotations from the unpublished diary of a sergeant-pilot reveal dismay at how the first daylight air raid (on January 12) was handled, "the big day" on which "our lads have been doing our best" but which, "thanks to the inability of lots of people to organize, train and run a fighter force" turned out to be "just a great big shambles" (1:293). The next day was also a bad one—"no organization, no leadership, no aircraft. Morale as low as it could be. . . . I wonder if I will be alive tomorrow" (1:296).

Throughout the last weeks of Singapore's resistance, a towering column of black smoke dominated the horizon, coming from the Navy's oil storage tanks. Pilots used it as a navigational aid, and as a landmark it appears in most of the panoramic photos Art Donahue shot during his time on the island. Oil was a major reason the British Empire was here, and its burning suggested that the old colonial aspirations were now the makings of a funeral pyre. It was also a major reason why the Japanese Empire was extending itself; the thought of an already militant enemy in command of such mighty resources was as chilling as the defenders' more immediate fates. Donahue finds himself among the few remaining pilots when, after most of the remaining Hurricanes are moved south to Sumatra (for what was claimed to be a crucial role defending Palembang and shipping in the Banka Straits), the last two flyable planes are moved from the overrun RAF fields to Kallang Airdrome, Singapore's municipal airport. "This was a sorry sight if there ever was one," he laments in *Last Flight from Singapore:*

> The road entering the airdrome passed under imposing stone archways, now pitifully scarred and chipped by blast and shrapnel and bullets. The beautiful hangars and terminal buildings of what had been a great airline base were barren and empty, with windows gone, walls gashed and torn. It reminded me of the buildings at Croydon Airdrome, London's great airline terminal, as they look today—deserted, because there are no airlines, with ticket and information booths silent and empty, windows blown in and walls shattered and scarred, results of the great mass bombing raid Croydon received in August 1940. (pp. 51-52)

The domestic scene is disconcerting for just the opposite reason. Donahue's quarters are at the lavish Sea View Hotel, as yet untouched by war, and the room he's given is furnished as if for a movie star, "a strange lair from which to go forth into battle" (p. 53). Dinner is seven courses, and breakfast is taken on the cool veranda, where the pilots sit "nonchalantly discussing how we should go about the bizarre and unearthly business that might occur in that other eerie world miles above us before the morning was out, while ordinary civilian men and women lounged around us, finishing their coffee, reading the morning papers, chatting as ordinary people anywhere might, not planning to kill anyone" (p. 58).

The only trouble comes from "one grumpy old codger" whose day of sipping pink gins at poolside is disturbed by some of the flyers splashing around after operations. They shouldn't be there, he insists, "because they hadn't been 'introduced'!" Cheerfully stating their names and shaking hands, the pilots "introduce" themselves and go on swimming (p. 71). Meanwhile a battery of guns answer the enemy's distant artillery, sounding "like two doors being slammed in another part of the building" (p. 89), and a lovely young English woman, as graceful as a dancer, exercises her two greyhounds on the lawn. "It seemed that either she or the approaching enemy and the terrible fighting must be unreal," Donahue ponders. "It just didn't make sense—but neither did a lot of things, in the last days of Singapore" (p. 90).

Because they were pilots, Donahue and the others escaped the city's fall, taking the fight on to bases in Sumatra. Among them, Terence Kelly remained incredulous that the fortress was being surrendered. In *Hurricane in Sumatra* (1991) he looks back on the Singapore experience and shares the amazement of the Japanese generals who were "astonished by the paucity of the resistance offered by an enemy which so outnumbered them" (p. 39). In *Hurricane and Spitfire Pilots at War* he makes the charge directly, that "we would fail but the fault would not be ours—the fault would lie at the doors of the incompetent commanders who lost us Singapore" (p. 117), and in *Hurricane over the Jungle* (1977) he generalizes that "Singapore, Sumatra and Java fell not because of any vast preponderance of men and arms by the Japanese but because the men who should and could have fought them off lost their courage, were bust in morale or were cowards" (pp. 47-48). As Churchill himself kept insisting, adequate numbers were surely there; even if all of the 100,000 plus personal on hand were not front-line soldiers, couldn't everyone at least hold a bayonet? Even the 50,000 British and Australian troops, supplemented by 20,000 native soldiers, outnumbered their attackers by far. Kelly's firsthand observations, recorded in *Hurricane over the Jungle*, show how little these numbers meant by January 29, when his squadron landed at Seletar airdrome and "within ten minutes of ordering a drink in the mess we realised that the pall of defeatism was so thick you could have cut it with a knife" (p. 49). In coming weeks he'd see nothing substantial to credit Japanese superiority. Their air raids were predictably by the clock, with airfield personnel strolling from the mess to eye the approaching formations, placing their beers at the trench's edge before taking shelter, then finishing off their brew before the bombers returned again same time next day; far from being a situation of panic, "it was clearly rather removed from Armageddon" (p. 48). As for the mighty naval guns being fixed in the wrong direction, the straits were not being crossed by capital ships but by sampans and bamboo rafts, targets for light artillery and even small arms rather than for the fortress's blockbusters. The problem, Kelly insists, was "the easy going, high flying way of life of both civilians and servicemen alike in the months and years before the war," an orientation that had made the reality of combat something unthinkable. Constructed as a fortress and successful as a kingpost of empire, Singapore was expected to remain that way, as if by definition. "Morale is an elusive quality which depends above everything else on leadership and example and without which it is hardly anything different from a ship without an engine or rudder which is blown by the winds of rumours and drifts in the currents of despair" (p. 53). After the war, Kelly would become a playwright, so his sense of motivations for these fey colonialists is well explained, but he also has a managerial understanding, which blames "the intermingling in an active theatre of war of mainly executive class civilians and servicemen" as unhelpful (pp. 53-54).

A specific complaint against leadership is made by several pilots. In *Chasing After Danger* Terence O'Brien describes how disastrous it was not to be used, a consequence of the Singapore leadership's obsession with preservation. "Those who wish to fight become frustrated and angry, rebellious against an authority that denies them use of a fighting machine when its need is clearly desperate" (p. 217), he confesses, establishing that for the entire month before mid-February's surrender full aircraft strength and crew capability were never employed, with night searches neglected and sorties against the Japanese forces assembling on the mainland never even considered. Hence, to the prevalent defeatism could be added the decay of aggressive morale. Terence Kelly's several books repeat how, whereas as many as a hundred Hurricanes could have inflicted severe casualties on a Japanese air force already stretched beyond prudent limits, this strength was "dribbled away piecemeal" (*Hurricanes and Spitfire Pilots at War*, p. 107) and only used in "penny numbers" (fewer than twelve [*Hurricane over the Jungle*, p. 56; *Hurricane in Sumatra*, p. 22]), the inevitable consequence of which was their one-by-one destruction. The madness of this strategy cries for protest, and protest eventually was voiced by an American in Kelly's squadron soon after it had been withdrawn from Singapore to Sumatra:

> Cardell Kleckner was a huge, tall American from Florida, a wide eyed man with a splendid laugh and a tremendous personality, a man with the way about him and the temerity to stroll, hand outstretched out on to the tarmac when General Wavell [the British theater commander] en route by Liberator from Singapore to Australia landed at Palembang to refuel, and to keep the great man chatting in the blazing sun until the job was done.
>
> "General," Kleckner had said wagging a finger at him while we gaped. "May I have a word with you." And Wavell had let him have his word, or many words—all about why we were going to lose Singapore, what we should have done in Singapore and where we went wrong in Singapore.
>
> And Wavell had listened attentively and been heard to answer, and more than once, "Thank you very much. That's a very good point you've made."
>
> And when it was all over Kleckner had wound up, "Well, Sir, nice to have met you" and by then the Liberator was refuelled and Wavell didn't even make it to the terminal building.
>
> But by the evening of February 4th, Kleckner . . . was dead, power diving, engine roaring, straight in. (*Hurricane over the Jungle*, pp. 70-71)

Another American, Art Donahue, was to follow Kelly and Kleckner to Palembang as the last RAF pilot to leave the collapsing fortress. Without a commanding general to

Last Allied view of Singapore and its burning oil storage tanks, taken from the cockpit of Art Donahue's Hurricane fighter. (Courtesy of Robert Donahue)

Flight Lieutenant Arthur G. Donahue, an American volunteer in the Royal Air Force and veteran of the Battle of Britain and the Fall of Singapore. (Courtesy of Robert Donahue)

berate and without any specific thesis to argue, his commentary that gives the title to *Last Flight from Singapore* stands as a conversation with himself. As his squadron was withdrawn from one airfield to another, he had always been left with the token remaining force, in this last case just two Hurricanes stationed at the municipal airport. Now, driven by Japanese rifle fire, he hurries to take off, and as he completes the circuit is shot at by enemy antiaircraft guns—over his own field, he notes with ironic dismay. At safe altitude he circles the city, taking photographs that he presumes will be the last air pictures of Singapore from someone on his side. These photos grace the endpapers of his book, but just as valuable are the thoughts he recalls from this moment, the last notes taken by any defender who would have another chance to fight:

> My final memory of Singapore, as it appeared to me looking back for the last time, is of a bright green little country, resting on the edge of the bluest sea I'd ever seen, lovely in the morning sunlight except where the dark tragic mantle of smoke ran across its middle and beyond, covering and darkening the city on the seashore.
> The city itself, with huge leaping red fires in its north and south parts, appeared to rest on the floor of a vast cavern formed by the sinister curtains of black smoke which rose from beyond and towered over it, prophetically, like a great overhanging cloak of doom. (p. 99)

From Sumatra, Donahue and his colleagues undertook a defense that was only slightly less fated to fail, fighting on thanks to a second airfield that was unnoted on maps and hence secret from the Japanese. Air Vice-Marshal P.C. Maltby, also in retreat from Singapore, addressed his men to say that Sumatra would be held to the end, winning back the RAF's good name even if it meant putting everyone from pilots to cooks in the front lines. This did not impress the flyers—not even their leader, Wing Commander J.R. Jeudwine, who in the second volume of *Bloody Shambles* regrets that Maltby "had no conception of the conditions under which we were operating, which precluded shaving every day and keeping our buttons polished" (p. 75). It did not help that immediately

Art Donahue's Hurricane fighter being serviced on Sumatra.
(Courtesy of Robert Donahue)

after his speech the air vice-marshal took off for Java, where by February 16 everyone else would be obliged to follow, given that Japanese paratroops had secured Palembang

Yet the RAF's Hurricane squadrons accomplished some real fighting in Sumatra, for once in this campaign. Closely packed Japanese invasion boats and barges were strafed by Hurricanes, a tactic that was gruesomely effective. In *Last Flight from Singapore* the episode inspires Art Donahue's best writing—not just because aggressive action is (for once) involved but because for a moment the RAF's best spirit has been revived. "It was the first time we'd taken off in squadron formation since we came to the Far East," he boasts. "I felt we must be making a magnificent show as we roared up over the boundary of the field all together, and climbed away into the northeast" (p. 138). Sighting the invasion force, Donahue is excited all the more, for "this was one of *the* moments for which we had been sent halfway around the world!" (p. 139). The shoot up is brutal but personally abstract. "There's nothing to it, really—you just press in with your thumb," even though one is firing right into the enemy's easily visible faces (p. 141). But before the author can consider this spectacle, he is hit himself, suffering a serious leg wound which nearly prevents him from guiding his plane back to base. Terence Kelly flies a similar mission just preceding Donahue's but regrets that the only offensive action is being taken by a handful of British, Commonwealth, and American pilots—the Dutch, he believed, were resigned from the start to accepting Japanese domination and assuming it would mean no more than different postage stamps and rules for commerce, unless the nations represented by his RAF squadron stepped in and changed the outcome. He could see that the casualities being inflicted on the Japanese advance force were horrendous; later, as their prisoner of war, he heard so many stories about this massacre from his captors that he hid his flying brevet in defense. "Yet we were ordered to evacuate to Java," he writes in *Hurricane in Sumatra.* "I think the answer has to be that the sense of panic generally prevailing clouded calm and reasoned judgement for there was still not one Japanese soldier within forty or fifty miles" (p. 121). Even when paratroops landed at Palembang and sealed off the RAF's first airfield, the wing commander managed a coup over the enemy forces demanding his surrender. As told in several memoirs, including Donahue's and Kelly's, this RAF officer confounded the Japanese by demanding that *they* surrender to *him*, leading to some confused conferencing behind the lines during which the Palembang squadron escaped. It was not for lack of aggressive spirit or ingenuity that the RAF had to leave Sumatra. "Unless a cool, unshakeable decision to resist, however bloody the battle might prove to be, was to be taken the moment that the [paratroop] drop had been reported," the author of *Hurricane in Sumatra* decides, "a moral vacuum filled with rumour and exaggeration was bound to ensue. And this is exactly what occurred. Both airfield and oilfield were evacuated not because the Japanese had seized them but because the enemy's mythical reinforcements rendered the defenders' positions untenable" (p. 145).

Sumatra could have been Japan's first reverse; something crucial when Kelly considers how the Pacific War was not one of ebb and flow, of victories mixed with defeats, but of steady forward momentum—which, when broken for the Japanese, "never gathered pace again" (p. 149). He makes another analogical argument for holding Java. Kelly suggests similarities between the Germans and Japanese positions in *Hurricane over the Jungle*. Just as Germany lost the Battle of Britain in large part by having to fly long distances to and from the field of operations, being thus short of fuel and limited by how long they could fight, and being unable to land damaged aircraft quickly or recover pilots who had bailed out:

> Exactly the same conditions would have applied to the Japanese who could only have attacked from Palembang several hundred miles to the north or from vulnerable aircraft carriers operating in an area subject to sudden and fierce tropical storms. Sumatra could have been a nasty thorn in the side of the Japanese but Java might have held. It was the one possible base for operations on a grand scale granted time to prepare; fought for tenaciously it had the size and terrain to absorb reverses; its southern coast was never for long a Japanese sea. A spirited air of resistance which would have been apparent to the native troops who fought with varying degrees of courage and to the Dutch who never, with the honourable exception of their Navy, fought at all might have helped build a different attitude. (p. 130)

Yet difference in attitude is the key, for nowhere in either the larger strategies of the Far East air war or the participants' memoirs resulting from that conflict is there an orientation comparing to the one that continued to fight at odds when Britain had its back to the wall. This is so not because of any lack of skill or courage, but rather because in Singapore, Sumatra, Java, and eventually Burma there was no wall to back up against, just the limitless expanse of space that separated England from her far-flung colonies. It is ironic to find one of Kelly's squadron mates in *Hurricane and Spitfire Pilots at War* "reading a book about Cobber Kain" (p. 113), the Battle of France hero of Noel Monks's *Squadrons Up!* (1940), because everything regarding both Kain and the style of book that tells his story is so radically different from what was transpiring in the Far East.

Not that the RAF memoirists don't try to find analogies—in his *Last Flight from Singapore* Art Donahue compares the strain of constant flying to Battle of Britain days when operating from Hawkinge and links the heroic ground crews at Singapore's ravaged Kallang Aerodrome to their embattled cousins back at RAF Manston, the air base closest to the Luftwaffe's fields in occupied France. By 1941 and 1942, of course, the Battle of Britain was being perceived as a great victory, and so ultimately even the most sincere comparisons between it and what was happening in the Far East break down. The Battle of France would seem to be a more useful model, from Fighter Command's refusal to commit additional squadrons (no Spitfires were sent) to the inevitability of complete withdrawal. "It was France all over again" (p. 160), Kenneth Hemingway writes in *Wings over Burma*, when resistance is suspended in favor of the necessary defense of India; as civilians flee from Rangoon to India, it reminds Bunny Stone of French peasants cramming the roads in flight from the German army's advance.

But even in the Battle of France there was room for optimism, albeit of the quixotically defiant nature. In *Squadrons Up!* Cobber Kain flies his Hurricane with brave abandon, an important element for Monks's characterization of how fighter pilots are so different from their counterparts in bombers. "Bomber pilots, with a crew of four or five dependent on their skill and judgment, have to be serious-minded," the journalist explains. "One reckless act, and five or six lives pay forfeit instead of one." On the other hand, and so important for the spirit in a war where at the time RAF fighters rather than bombers are the key element, "In the fighter pilot recklessness is a virtue. Fighting alone in his flying bullet, he can afford to be reckless. It gets him out of tight corners at times" (p. 37). As the RAF's first popular hero, Kain is seen achieving this success by his wild, exuberant style of flying and fighting—absolutely necessary attributes considering the Luftwaffe's great superiority. That the Battle of France is lost matters no more to Britain's spirit than the fact

that Kain himself dies when the book ends, taking a fare-
well fling in his Hurricane before being posted back to England and, as he shows off some daring aerobatics, losing
control and diving into the ground. What a flamboyantly
romantic way to go—so different from the Empire's overly
cautious husbanding of forces and ignominious retreat before even facing an enemy they actually outnumbered. "All
right, then—alone!" read the defiant caption on the political
cartoon depicting a fist-shaking British serviceman on the
south coast beaches railing against an enemy now in control
of everything but England itself. The way the RAF was used
in the Far East allowed no such rallying sentiment.

The most evident contrast in attitudes is found in the
different styles of memoirs Art Donahue and Barry Sutton
wrote before and after their Far East experience. Each had
been Battle of Britain pilots, Sutton fighting in the Battle of
France as well, and their initial stories reflect the better spirit
of the air war being fought from England. Donahue's *Tally-
Ho! Yankee in a Spitfire* starts with a rousing title and never
loses its enthusiasm for a good fight being especially well
fought. All of the typical American-in-the-RAF themes are
there, from the humor of his countrymen playing so insou-
ciantly with Royal Air Force custom to the high esteem in
which the British people hold these gallant volunteers. His
action descriptions are high spirited, and when listening to
an interception overhead while recovering from injuries in
a hospital the author's imagination is able to vitalize, even
sensualize the scene:

> I would be listening to the humming of a Daimler-Benz
> cruising, and the *rhoom-rhoom* of a Rolls Royce turning pretty
> fast: and all at once there would be the roar of guns from a
> Spitfire or Hurricane. That would be answered instantly by the
> quick crescendo of the Daimler-Benz changing from its normal
> cruising right up the scale to its most agonized whine, over the
> space of about a second, as the surprised Nazi pilot "pushed
> everything forward" and opened up with every ounce of his
> engine's power to get away. The response was similar to what
> you get from stepping on the tail of a cat. (pp. 78-79)

Sutton's *The Way of a Pilot* in much similar manner conforms with all the traditions of early British air war narratives. Like many of them, it is written while its author is recovering from combat injuries, in Sutton's case burns suffered in his shot-up Hurricane's cockpit before he could bail out. As he looks back on what has brought him to this point, Sutton touches on all the familiar facets of fighter-pilot lore: a love of speed, a fine aesthetic appreciation of beautiful prewar planes such as the Hawker Hind and Hart, and the understanding of how in both sport and glory his style of warfare above the clouds surpasses unpleasantries on the ground. There is a feeling of sympathy for his Luftwaffe victims, born of kinship in the air, but most of all a firm grasp of what he is doing and why, a sensation evident in his book's penultimate episode when he is almost shot down by a Messerschmitt 109:

> Heading home at last, I became aware of a strange emotion I had never known before.
>
> I have since been in tighter corners, been much more conscious of danger and perhaps become more casual with the experience, but that feeling of supreme elation, almost lightheadedness, has never left me immediately after a battle.
>
> I slid back the roof of the cockpit, put my seat in its proper notch, and took a deep breath of the fresh air. Looking over the side, I thought the fields of Kent had never looked more green. Crossing over the Estuary, I looked towards the west—surely the setting sun had never smiled so genially through the smoking sky-line of London.
>
> I began to sing. (p. 105)

Neither Sutton's subsequent *Jungle Pilot* nor Donahue's *Last Flight from Singapore* enthuses with sentiments like these. Looking back on his experience in Burma, Sutton rues how it is not the excitement of operations he remembers any more than the chess games played during rest periods with a colleague. "It is something more," he recalls, "something which may be now difficult to explain. Perhaps it was the one unspoken truth that we were fighting a losing battle" (p. 84). True, France had been a losing battle as well, but not in the way Burma presented itself. In Burma instead of bold recklessness and heroic gestures against an iron-crossed enemy of mighty Teutonic knights, Sutton and his pilots had simply tried "to stop a swarm of locusts with a few flit guns" (p. 85). When Rangoon is about to fall and its oil wells are put to the torch, "the firelight proclaimed a message of despair and wrote it across the heavens." So different from his departure from France, when it was so clear that the real fight lay ahead in a context that the RAF much preferred, prematurely abandoning Rangoon prompts Sutton to do what a good fighting man should never do: interrogate his purpose. "Did the sight of those fires at a time like this mean only one thing to all of us?" he asks. "The negation of all our efforts? So then it certainly seemed to me" (p. 86).

Sutton's despair comes near the end of his second memoir, but Donahue's is voiced from the first page of *Last Flight from Singapore*, where as opposed to the sense of purpose guiding his *Tally Ho! Yankee in a Spitfire* he can now regret how "my accomplishments in the Far East proved to be so small and my attempts at accomplishment so regularly crowned with frustration, that there could hardly have been any design about it." As opposed to such rewarding service in the Battle of Britain, this young American was now party to "the greatest military disaster ever suffered by British arms." By the end of his adventures, he is "sad, too, and spiritually very tired," with "no need denying that I was terribly disillusioned by much of what I had seen and experienced out here—things I have avoided or passed over in this story because it isn't in my province as a member of the forces to speak of them, and because I could only do harm by telling about them now [in 1942]. The enemy don't advertise their failings either, you know" (p. 153).

Yet the failings of this entire theater were everywhere to be seen. Preparation had been lax, attitudes were unrealistic, planning was unnecessarily abstract, reinforcements were extremely slim, and command bordered on the inept. It is not surprising that spirit would fail, completing the vicious circle of despair and defeat. Above all, it was a different style of conflict, one not to be decided by beautifully crafted machines flown by chivalrous adversaries over the English Channel and the hop fields of Kent but by land armies of different races and vastly different cultures with little knowledge and even less appreciation for each other. In *Hurricane and Spitfire Pilots at War,* Terence Kelly notes, "This was a sly, stealthy war, a mean war fought in the mud and slime of foetid jungles, under the cover of dense overgrowth, by two opposing armies each of whose total strength was considerable but which, for the most part, operated in small units" (p. 140). Being able to fight in the skies rather than on the ground failed to make it more attractive, for being shot down did not mean parachuting into a Kentish haystack, being plucked from a dinghy in a twenty-two-mile-wide Channel, or being hidden by French resistance fighters before being spirited back to England, all of which happened again and again and again, but bailing out or coming down in the most atrocious conditions imaginable. Whether in Malaya, Sumatra, or Burma, RAF pilots faced a geography and ecosphere far different from anything previously experienced. "In some of the earth's most inhospitable terrain, such as icy mountains or raging seas or burning deserts, you can imagine means of survival," Terence O'Brien allows in *Chasing After Danger,* "but nothing on earth I have ever seen offered less hope than that dark steamy jungle swamp, and no death more frightening than the lingering horrors it threatened" (p. 177).

Beautifully written aerial descriptions are a rarity in RAF memoirs from the Far East. The makings for picturesque literature are on the ground—and all of it, from the riotous color of flowers and other vegetation to the splendor of the colonial way of living, is simply a trap for unsuspecting attitudes and an indication of how things have been allowed to go so terribly wrong. It is appropriate, therefore, that when the skeptical Terence Kelly lets himself loose for a moment to depict the aesthetic pleasures of a combat adventure in the air he nearly brings himself to grief.

The passage in question comes near the end of *Hurricane over the Jungle,* when the last shred of his squadron is flying against the Japanese from its last base in Java:

> It was a day of towering cumulus and our attack was made on a circle of Navy Os orbiting within a chasm between two such

cloud formations. I happened to be the first to peel off and having passed through the Japanese I steepened almost to the vertical, engine full bore, and looked back on the off chance of seeing if I'd had any luck. And I saw one of the most beautiful things I ever saw flying. Following me down were the other three and after them was peeling the whole formation of Navy Noughts. Every aircraft was sharp and clear against the background of white cumulus. It was like a film set but gigantic in scale, the actors miniscule but giving life to it—twenty, thirty aircraft all in a screaming vertical power dive against a pure white background with the green and red of the land hurtling upwards and the blue above. It was quite unforgettable. (p. 138)

Unforgettable but also quite futuristic, for soon Kelly realizes that he has watched it far too long and is now about to experience something that would become part of postwar air lore, breaking the sound barrier.

Here, too, all the familiar parts of aviation writing fall into line: the frozen controls, buffeting wing surfaces, shriekings of wind and engine, and the earth rushing up from below. Then, too, there is the calm, rational pilot, a model Chuck Yeager would make so famous after the war and that would become a staple of movies from *Breaking the Sound Barrier* to *The Right Stuff* a generation later—the state of mind, as Kelly puts it, in which "you understand very clearly the predicament you're in and that if you don't find a way out of it quickly you will soon be dead" (p. 139). His critical thinking comes to the rescue, and by using the Hurricane's sturdy trim tabs he manages to bring his plane out of its nearly 180° dive. Once more straight and level, he's astounded to see that his air speed is 590 miles per hour, and concludes that moments before he could well have exceeded the speed of sound.

In the era of peace that followed, such adventures would replace air combat as materials for the most vivid aviation memoirs. For now, in these words written about an episode coming just days before the RAF's withdrawal, Terence Kelly epitomizes the radical change that would overtake Britain and the empire he had been sent here to defend. Indefensible it proved to be, and even after the land was retaken in the long, slow, tedious advances of 1943, 1944, and 1945, Britain's hold on these outposts was extremely tenuous. By 1947 even India, from which the reconquest was launched, would be independent. Like crashing through the sound barrier, the postwar years would provide an entirely different world for Britain to cope with, turning away from two centuries of empire to prepare for a new millennium in orientation with Europe. None of this was evident to flyers in the Battle of Britain, but the picture seemed all too clear to those who fought in Far Eastern skies during the last month of 1941 and the first quarter of 1942.

An
Adventurers'
War

– • – By the end of spring 1942, Singapore and its environs to the south plus Burma had been taken by the Japanese. The Flying Tigers and, after July 4, regular United States Army Air Force units would fight on from China, their original destination, while the Royal Air Force would regroup in India and begin a different style of operations (largely ground attack and air supply) toward the retaking of Burma and points east. As opposed to the swiftness of Japan's assault against ragtag, disorganized, and sometimes dispirited defenses, the new allies' advance was painfully slow. Deliberate as it was against a strong, deeply entrenched military force, this campaign was conducted in a different spirit from that which had characterized the war's first phase. But activities in the China-Burma-India theater, as it was now called, still distinguished themselves from other theaters of operations. Weather and terrain remained unique threats to the ill-supplied and differently equipped forces flying in such conditions. And the men who did the flying remained something of a different breed.

In several ways this much longer second portion of the war that still wasn't first reflected Western aviation's earliest interest in the Far East. When something is not a priority, it tends to operate by its own rules rather than by the regimen where crucial matters are at stake. A different type of pilot may be drawn there; without doubt, only a different kind of aviator working under such conditions could succeed.

In looking over how the Far East air war was resolved, it is helpful to consider the nature of American and British participation in the region as much as ten years before, for there is a great continuity in styles. By 1937, for example, Royal Leonard had already been in China for a year and a half and had risen in employment from flying the Young Marshal on his warlord adventures to working as the personal pilot of Generalissimo Chiang Kai-shek. In *I Flew for China*, there is a remarkable scene where, just after the Marco Polo Bridge incident on July 7, 1937, Leonard is surprised to meet another of Chiang's new hires, the man who had taught this commercial adventurer to fly during his military training at Kelly Field in 1923. Hearing a knock at his door at Nanking's Metropolitan Hotel, Leonard responds to find "a stocky, leather-faced man with grizzled hair and sharp black eyes. He was dressed in unpressed flannels and a leather jacket." He's recognized immediately. "For the love of Mike," Leonard exclaims, "Come on in, Chennault!" (p. 116). Chiang has brought both men here for a reason: to consider whether Japan's act of war should be treated as such. Leonard's response, published in July 1942 just as the USAAF took over what had been an exceedingly irregular war, is typical of how matters were arranged in the Orient:

> We started to discuss the sad condition of the Chinese air force. The picture was certainly not encouraging. The Chinese lacked almost everything—pilots, planes, training, guns—all that goes into making a first-class aviation group. I could see Chennault's jaw harden as I told him this.
>
> "Well," he said, "there are a bunch of American flyers around. Maybe we can do something." (pp. 116-17)

When the Colonel's jaw hardens, one sees his classic portrait and the impression by which most who ever met him anchored their descriptions. And the act of setting it matches perfectly with what is being said, as if a stern visage and a few American pilots can make a difference. Though springing from an entirely different culture, British attitudes toward what could be done in the Far East at times coincided. Though overshadowed and overpowered by colonial dispositions that had nothing to do with air power at all, a similar feistiness could be found in the flyers who stood and fought. Once they saw the nimble Nakajima Ki-27 Nates flitting like gnats around their more powerful though less maneuverable Hurricanes, British pilots guessed that one of the planners' supposedly sick jokes—that obsolete Gloster Gladiator biplanes be sent to Singapore—might have indeed worked if tried. After all, just three of these little antique aircraft had defended Malta until reinforcements could be sent. As for adventuring in China, that was a potential destination as well for flyers subsequently famous in the RAF. Johnny Kent thought of going there in the early 1930s to help the Chinese Air Force fight the Japanese in Manchuria. Instead, he left his native Canada to join the Royal Air Force in England, where he rose to command 303 Squadron in the Battle of Britain—a squadron made up mostly of Polish airmen who'd fled their own country's collapse. One of the most famous of these was a flight lieutenant named Witold A. Urbanowicz, who after shooting down seventeen German planes was assigned as the assistant Polish air attaché in Washington, D.C. Allegedly "too famous" to return to combat status with the RAF, Urbanowicz pulled diplomatic strings and managed to get an observer's assignment to China, trusting that in his unorthodoxy Chennault might give him a job. By the winter of 1943-44 Urbanowicz, now a major in the USAAF, flew combat missions with the 75th Fighter Squadron. "A bunch of American flyers around"? Before the war's end, this line would have been expanded well past any credibility likely in 1937, given all that happened with the American Volunteer Group, the RAF's consideration of helping out the AVG, and Urbanowicz's postwar choice of American citizenship.

Of course in the China-India-Burma theater there were other types around as well, some of whom went in the opposite direction. There were Germans in China that Royal Leonard had to deal with, some of them quite famous, in-

cluding Eric Just, an ace from Baron Manfred von Richt–
hofen's World War I fighter squadron, and Captain Walther
Stennes, the head of Chiang's personal bodyguard unit, who
in 1938 sat Leonard down for a stern lecture:

> "You Americans are damned fools!" he said. "You should
> realize that you cannot hold the Philippines. You should realize
> that Japan wants your blood even more than the blood of the
> British. I give you this warning now, my friend! Tell it to some
> army officers you know. In a few years it will be too late!"
> Stennes, who originally fled from Nazi Germany because he
> opposed Hitler (he commanded the German army squad that
> locked Hitler up in 1923), has gone back to what he believes is
> the winning side. He is now [1942] head of the Gestapo in
> Shanghai. (p. 142)

Yet for every German who made a wrong choice, there were
a hundred Americans who profited from a good decision,
among them a German-American adventurer named Albert
"Ajax" Baumler. Baumler already had tangled with Nazis—
not Hitler and his inner circle directly, but with Luftwaffe
pilots in the Condor Legion flying for Franco's revolution-
aries in Spain. As a Loyalist pilot during the Spanish Civil
War, he had downed eight German and Italian planes and
was one of Chennault's top picks for the AVG. It took him
until April 1942 to get there, but he stayed to become commander of the USAAF's 74th Fighter Squadron; one of the
first targets he'd personally attack would be the Gia Lam
Airdrome in Hanoi, well known to another generation of
American pilots a quarter century and two wars later.

By the time American and British operations were over
in the Far East, a stellar cast of characters had played roles
in this theater. Some of them were important Air Corps
careerists, such as General Caleb Haynes, who commanded
Chennault's new USAAF bomber forces. Because Haynes
had most recently directed the Army Air Force's Transport
Command, Radio Tokyo repeatedly taunted this pioneer of
the four-engine bomber as being "the old broken-down transport pilot." As Robert L. Scott reports in *God Is My Co-Pilot*,
Haynes responded with propaganda of his own, printing
up thousands of multilingual leaflets reading "COMPLI-

MENTS OF THE OLD BROKEN-DOWN TRANSPORT PI-
LOT" and dropping them on each mission—some tied to
bombs, others falling from the bomb bays, and still more
tossed out over Japanese-occupied cities after his planes had
made their attack (pp. 222-23). Others were prominent figures from American life, such as Chennault's first official
chief of staff, Colonel Merian C. Cooper. A heroic World War
I flyer, Cooper had fought on by helping lead the Kosciusko
Squadron in the Polish-Russian war that followed. Afterward, he became an explorer on three continents and went
on to become a Hollywood producer, having a hand in *King
Kong* and other classics. World War II brought him back into
the service working for Air Corps Intelligence in Washington, D.C., but like so many other colorful characters he
yearned for Chennault's action in China. Joe Alsop was back
there as well, having talked his way out of internment in
Japanese-held Hong Kong. In one case, prominence would
emerge only much later and be discovered well after that, as
in the story Scott tells in *The Day I Owned the Sky*. On his own
way to China, the author's unit had adopted a local officer's
son as an unofficial mascot. Decades after the war, Scott
would make an otherwise impossible visit to what was now
Pakistan thanks to some curious intervention at the top; only
later, after the man's tragic execution, was it learned that the
one-time mascot named "Ali" had grown up to be the
country's prime minister, Zulfikar Ali Bhutto (pp. 143-44).

Surely the most colorful (and at times outrageous) adventurers in this Far East air war were the improbable trio
of Harvey Greenlaw, his wife Olga, and Greg "Pappy"
Boyington. As Chennault's unofficial chief staff officer,
Greenlaw was capping a life of Oriental adventuring, having resigned an Army Air Corps commission in 1932 to ac-
company the Jouett aviation mission to the Chinese
government and returning again to represent the North
American Aviation Company in its dealings with Chiang Kai-
shek's air force. When he joined the American Volunteer
Group, Olga became the unit's official diarist, in addition to
taking notes for her own memoir, *The Lady and the Tigers*,
published in 1943. Boyington, of course, was the AVG's most

notorious pilot, but from both *Baa Baa Black Sheep* and *Tonya*, published in 1958 and 1960, respectively, it was clear that he was in Harvey's hair (and in Olga's bed) as often as he was tangling alternately with Chennault and the Japanese.

Only in the movies could a character like Olga Greenlaw be imagined with any real credibility. As it was, her appearance and behavior in the Far East air war were fantastic to describe, as Wing Commander Bunny Stone recounts in his part of Bush Cotton's *Hurricanes over Burma*: "There was a frightful row of a battle going on overhead when, to our astonishment, a bejewelled goddess appeared through the door, looking as if she had just stepped from a New York or Paris salon." It was Olga, and though her husband continued with his briefing to the RAF, "we found it hard to concentrate" (p. 294). In *The Lady and the Tigers*, Olga maintains this image, forever throwing little snits (like Scarlett O'Hara in *Gone with the Wind*'s movie version) and remarking that when fleeing Japanese bombardments she'd simply grab her most vital possession, an Elizabeth Arden makeup kit. She further plays up the feminine by having long heart-to-heart talks and developing sentimental attachments to pilots who will soon die, a habit Pappy Boyington makes much fun of in *Tonya*. As for Harvey Greenlaw, Boyington makes him an impotent martinet in both books, a pathetic character forever threatening to court-martial everyone and having no idea whatsoever that his much younger and quite beautiful wife has become the tramp of the outfit, memoir and novel replicating such scenes:

> Harvey Greenlaw, the self-made executive officer, called himself Lieutenant Colonel Greenlaw, although no one else would. The manner in which Harvey was forever talking courts-martial to threaten a group of civilians gave me the impression that he must have been at least one jump ahead of a few himself in his military days. The poor guy gave the impression that he hated everybody. Maybe Harvey had his reasons. Who knows? (*Baa Baa Black Sheep*, p. 43)
>
> . . . . .
>
> "Yes sir." With a sharp salute, Auggie [as he is called fictively] jumped into his jeep and started driving about the area like an

ant on a red hot stove, ordering each man officiously. "You'll
report to the clubhouse at exactly 1100. Failure to do so will
result in a court-martial."

"Where in hell does he get this court-martial crap?" a
crewman snarled after Auggie had departed. "We're
civilians, not servicemen, under a year's contract like any
other employee."

"The bastard hates everybody, including himself," another
crewman observed. "Must have nightmares of facing general
courts in his brilliant past." (*Tonya*, p. 31)

Boyington himself remains the essentially harmless bad
boy, being threatened with one of Greenlaw's courts-mar-
tial for engaging in a rickshaw race (where he and a colleague pulled the Burmese drivers in their own vehicles) and
doing no worse in the air than having his section of five P-
40s run out of gas and crash land near the Indo-China border, even then returning to salvage three of the five and
managing to fly them out, a piece of brilliant airmanship
that impressed Frank Losonsky as noted in the latter's *Flying Tiger: A Crew Chief's Story*. Of course, both actions proved
rather unnecessary points; the rickshaw exploit was supposedly an exercise in cross-cultural, translingual relations,
whereas for all the great bravado in flying the planes from
an airstrip hacked out of the jungle, "We could have easily
'hauled' them back to Kunming," as Losonsky notes (p. 86).

Others drawn to the Far East had higher motives and
responded in a better spirit to what they saw. Donald S.
Lopez's *Into the Teeth of the Tiger* describes a flight from
Kunming to Assam that stops to refuel at Gaya, a place that
for Lopez was "just another airstrip to me until a few years
ago when my son, a professor of eastern religions, told me
that Gaya was where, some five hundred years before Christ,
Siddartha Gautama attained the enlightenment that made
him the Buddha and founded one of the world's great religions" (p. 118). Robert L. Scott, the first of the regular Air
Force pilots to make a name for himself in China (as the first
commander of the 23rd Fighter Group, the AVG's immediate successor), once flew a mission that took him over the
Great Wall of China; since childhood he had been haunted
by a picture of the Wall, and after retiring from a long Air

Force career he made an almost impossible return to a country not yet reopened to the West and walked this same almost inaccessible portion, a journey celebrated in *The Day I Owned the Sky*. Just getting to China the first time had been a major challenge, struggling with the Air Corps for combat status, taking a Transport Command post (for which he had to fake multiengine qualifications) to get as far as India, and then wrangling a P-40 from Chennault himself (by showing how he could get a supposedly unserviceable plane off the ground in an air raid).

With his own fighter, Scott began freelancing as a one-man escort to the otherwise undefended transports and as an occasional intruder into enemy airspace. He'd tune his radio to the AVG's band and listen eagerly to their communications, learning tactics as he eavesdropped but mostly just experiencing the vicarious thrill of pretending to be a Flying Tiger. His greatest service to the group was how he took personal initiative to change General Clayton Bissell's supply priorities, dumping his tons of paperwork in the jungle and reloading with vitally needed war stuffs. When he finally met some AVG pilots during a lull in the fighting—in a scene right out of an RAF flyer's Wild West imagination, akin to a new U.S. marshal being cold shouldered by a cowboy town's vigilantees—he won them over not with tales of his own fighter prowess but by explaining how he'd reformed their supply line.

One of the best endorsements of Robert L. Scott comes from James H. Howard as noted in the latter's *Roar of the Tiger* (1991). Howard was an exceptional personality himself, the child of missionaries to China who by being raised there had a special understanding of the country and its people. He flew both in China with Chennault and then from England as part of the equally famous Mustang squadrons in the 354th Fighter Group, single-handedly attacking thirty Messerschmitts and downing three while driving the others away (an achievement that had journalists calling him a "one-man air force"). Of Scott's freelancing he has this to say:

> The next air officer to come through was Col. Bob Scott.

Scott had borrowed a Kittyhawk from Chennault while he was still assigned to stagnant staff duties with the Tenth Air Force in India. His urge to get into action had prompted him to carry out some spectacular one-man bombing and strafing missions against Japanese installations in Burma. He flew several missions with us [in the AVG], usually as a wingman to an element leader. Imagine, if you will, a full colonel flying the wing of a pilot who had been a second lieutenant less than a year before. Scott, in his humble way, said, "I consider it an honor to fly in a formation of pilots who have been tested in combat." (p. 157)

Whereas other regulars of the USAAF had been disliked and distrusted, this different style of man was warmly accepted. "Scott's enthusiasm and good humor appealed to all of us," Howard reports. "Needless to say we gave him the thumbs-up, and he became commander of the newly formed Twenty-Third Fighter Group, successor to the AVG" (p. 159).

Flying in China fulfilled a dream for Scott and led to lifetime ambitions later achieved with great panache. As a very young officer he'd dared the elements by flying the mail (in a pioneering experiment the dangers of which prompted the government not to continue with Air Corps personnel) and had undertaken a 14,000-mile trip by light motorcycle from France to Mount Ararat in Turkey, retracing part of Marco Polo's journey. In *God Is My Co-Pilot*, published to great acclaim in 1943 and released as a Warner Brothers motion picture early in 1945, he influenced wartime opinion supporting America's presence in China, just as his *Damned to Glory* (1944) helped build a legendary reputation for the otherwise maligned P-40. With *Flying Tiger: Chennault of China* (1959) Scott became one of his old boss's advocates at a time when cold war politics were heating up in military quarters. At times he could be lyrical, wondering at the psychological separation a flyer feels when leaving his own continent—no longer able, "in a pinch," to "walk home," as he writes in *God Is My Co-Pilot* (p. 59)—and marveling at how even a routine flight takes him far above territory "listed as 'unexplored and unadministered'" (p. 92) from which he can see both the Dalai Lama's palace and the common source of the five big rivers of Asia: the Irrawaddy, the Salween, the

Mekong, the Yangtze, and the Yellow. His present war would encompass the first two; subsequent conflicts would make the other three by-words in military reports. Most dramatically Scott distinguished himself in the air as both a courageous fighter and sharp tactician and on the ground as something a regular Army Air Force officer might never presume to be: a younger version of Chennault himself, defying bullheaded officers, standing up (on just the near side of insolence) to General Clayton Bissell, and being defended by Chennault to the extent of the latter threatening General Stilwell with a resignation submitted directly to President Roosevelt himself should his fighter commander be subjected to any type of reprimand at all.

The most colorful adventurer of all was Claire Lee Chennault. His autobiography, *Way of a Fighter*, catalogues a lifetime of combats well beyond the specifics of fighter aircraft. This was a man who had to fistfight his overgrown, scrappy country-school pupils, who had to fight his way into the sky as a trainee pilot and then fight the bomber adversaries throughout his frustrating career in the Air Corps, who had to battle against long-held custom and deeply entrenched interests to get a Chinese Air Force into even minimal shape, who struggled in Washington to get the American Volunteer Group formed and struggled all the more to get them trained and keep them in line, and who throughout his years of command in China faced conflict after conflict with his superiors (notably Bissell and Stilwell) in India, all the time working hard to keep relations with Generalissimo Chiang Kai-shek on an even keel. As a reward, he was retired soon after China had been secured but only a month before the Japanese surrender, prompting General MacArthur to study the otherwise complete ranks of commanders on board the USS *Missouri* in Tokyo Harbor and ask, "Where's Chennault?" Hence, after the war, as evidenced in his 1949 autobiography, he was still compelled to fight for the acknowledgment that all along he had been right.

There are obvious reasons why Claire Chennault was absent. Throughout his service career he had bucked the system, getting only more unmanageable as he reached the top, an ascendancy only possible during times of duress when the military needed his successes whatever the cost. At several points during the war he had made it clear that he'd be much more trouble to get rid of than to keep; Roosevelt had taken up the practice of writing him directly and encouraging the man's responses—and if direct appeal to the President failed, there was always the media to orchestrate, beginning with the Luce empire that had discovered his Flying Tigers as a newsworthy item back in 1941 and kept Chennault's exploits in the forefront of war reporting. But with the war almost over, such threats lost their power; brashly unconventional commanders might have been needed to fight the fight, but they were hardly necessary to keep the peace. Indeed, a loose cannon like Chennault could well be taken as a threat to continued security. And as the war wound down suspicions arose that this old fighter might be shifting targets in favor of a new enemy.

One of the many arguments between Chennault and Stilwell was over how closely the U.S. command should work with the Communist forces under Mao Tse-tung. Stilwell wanted more cooperation; Chennault, knowing how the Generalissimo had managed only a temporary and at times imperfectly executed rapprochement with his old adversaries, was increasingly wary of a Communist threat, both to Chiang and to American postwar interests. This controversy extended to high levels in both military strategy and Roosevelt administration policy and remained an issue well into the second half of the twentieth century. Most immediately, there was some belief that as the summer of 1945 continued Chennault was using his forces less to solidify Chiang's victory over the Japanese than to improve his position in relation to the Communist armies.

Within the boundaries of World War II, Chennault never had the chance. But in January 1946 he returned to China as a private citizen, just as he'd been in 1937 after his first retirement from U.S. military service, and at once began planning how to fight for what he felt China needed. For a cold war, weapons would be economic and tactics those of commerce, and he rightly construed that without a decent transportation system both China and Chiang's government within it would be helpless. And so he returned to the United States and undertook a mission similar in many respects to his formation of the AVG. This time the initials were CAT, standing for Civil Air Transport, and the supporting power was not the U.S. government but the United Nations Relief and Rehabilitation Agency (UNRAA), directed by the aviation-minded former mayor of New York City, Fiorello La Guardia. Once again the organization was a commercial one, and the people involved included Chennault and a number of Roosevelt administration insiders and holdovers from the old days of China Defense Supplies. Many of its 1,100 flying and ground crew personnel were former Flying Tigers and veterans of the Fourteenth Air Force, the AVG's ultimate successor. An independent but parallel company formed by AVG pilot Bob Prescott to fly produce from the California Fruit Growers Association to China soon became known as the Flying Tiger Line, and so even the old mythical name was kept alive in this new style of Far East air adventuring.

The nature of Chennault's adventure became transparently anti-Communist. During the civil war that began in 1948, CAT C-46s and C-47s kept beseiged Nationalist cities supplied. In her *A Thousand Springs: The Biography of a Marriage* (1962), Anna Chennault places her husband's work with CAT in the context of his larger plans for the country:

> It was after George Marshall left China, blaming both sides for failure to achieve a coalition, that General Chennault realized that only a radical shift in American policy could now save China.
>
> In the hope that this might yet happen, he began a dramatic and effective fight for time. As the Reds swept south, he used the only physical weapon against Communism available to him—CAT, as an evacuation and supply line. The big transport planes carried no machine guns and their pilots made no attacks on the Reds. But the CAT personnel planes, unarmed, fought as bravely as the soldiers of Free China, and sometimes more effectively. (pp. 190-91)

As the airline's publicist, Anna Chennault worked on its retrospective image as well, emphasizing how "it acquired a personality reminiscent of the old AVG, the Flying Tigers" (p. 156). In her present book, she strives for continuity, tracing the AVG's spirit through the Fourteenth Air Force to CAT, where "its flame burned brightly still, sustained throughout by the fire of the man who had first inspired it, Claire Chennault." She adds that during this period several AVG and USAAF veterans urged their old General "to create another volunteer group to fight the Reds," something he declined to do, preferring "after years of using planes for destructive purposes to be able to use them in building up a country" (p. 261). In fact, Chennault spent much of July 1949, in Washington, D.C., lobbying for just such a plan. *Life* gave the appeal publicity and praised it as a great idea; Congress thought not, and President Truman was of a different mood toward China than had been Roosevelt.

Undaunted, Chennault returned to China in time to reestablish his CAT in Taiwan in the service of Chiang's exiled government, a story told best by Felix Smith in *China Pilot: Flying for Chiang and Chennault* (1995). With the outbreak of hostilities in Korea beginning in 1950, CAT became a contract hauler for the United States, transporting both cargo and troops. By 1954, CAT found a new customer in the government of France, which had Chennault's pilots dropping supplies to French troops at beseiged Dien Bien Phu. One of these flyers was AVG veteran Erik Shilling, who also flew missions along the coast of mainland China to monitor that nation's radar system. The nature of this work was so secret that Shilling was never sure for whom he was really working. "The French ignored the help given to them by American pilots," he writes in *Destiny*, "although we were Dien Bien Phu's only source of supply after the fall of the airfield" (p. 273). This program lasted two months and was flown in C-119 transports provided by the USAF. As Duane Schultz notes in *The Maverick War*, "One of Chennault's pilots, James McGovern, was shot down and killed on one of these missions, along with his co-pilot, Wallace Buford, and several French cargo handlers. They may have been America's first casualities in the long war in Vietnam" (p. 312). There might easily have been more, had not President Eisenhower quashed an idea Chennault was promoting to lobbyists and via feature articles in *Look*: that a 470-man force of volunteer American pilots be equipped with F-84 Thunderjets and begin fighting for the French.

As it happened, Chennault's legacy survived into the Vietnam era when his partners sold CAT to the CIA, which renamed it Air America as its own airline. One of these partners, Whiting Willauer, also remained active in the world of clandestine operations, planning great portions of the Bay of Pigs invasion of Cuba in 1961. Claire Chennault himself had died in 1958 from lung cancer. One of his last activities had been to leave his hospital bed for a photo shoot advertising a famous brand of cigarettes, saying he needed money for medical bills. Even at the very end, he was acting with such flamboyance as to make his work with the American Volunteer Group just one of many such acts in his death-defying adventurer's life.

Britain's air experience in the war that wasn't first did not yield figures as adventurously colorful as Claire Chennault—nor as outrageous as Pappy Boyington or inspiring as Robert L. Scott. Its bona fide heroes had achieved iconic status in a war that *was* first, both chronologically and by military priority: the Battle of Britain. What happened in Singapore and Burma was something to be forgotten, a "bloody shambles" in execution that as a military action was considered a disgraceful defeat and which even as eventual victory was achieved became a region where United Kingdom and United Nations aims were sometimes painfully distinct. If there was a figure to be cut, it was by Lord Louis Mountbatten, who was the first overall commander to bring effective order to the theater and who later, as the last viceroy of India, supervised the end of Britain's empire there when independence came in 1947.

It was during their regrouping at bases in India when flyers of the Royal Air Force began noting the anticolonial stirrings so evident to AVG members getting a first look at a colonial outpost in 1941. But from these same bases squadrons of Mohawks, Hurricanes, Beaufighters, and eventually Spitfires and Mosquitoes developed something revolutionary themselves: a radically new style of air war for the RAF that had them flying close support for slow, methodical ground advances back across the territory abandoned so hurriedly in the early months of 1942. It is significant that by the summer of 1944 this became a method for RAF fighter and fighter-bomber squadrons in Europe, as well, and led to the force's role in NATO planning afterward and execution in the Gulf War of 1991.

Another revolutionary element, at least as the RAF was concerned, involved contributing to a major offensive with air supply. The long march from India back across Burma was supplied entirely by air, the first such major campaign to depend exclusively on such logistical support. Like later wars, it could be directed from a great distance away: Mountbatten maintained his headquarters in Ceylon (today's Sri Lanka). In addition to keeping the advance of main ground forces moving, the RAF dropped the raiding columns of General Orde Wingate behind Japanese lines and kept them supplied in their marauding, disruptive activities—a thousand men doing a job as effectively as an entire division or more, all of it impossible without RAF Dakotas slipping in by moonlight to take out their sick and wounded and keep them going in ways that made the enemy believe they were much more potent than facts would have revealed. Here the USAAF chipped in as well, offering a dozen B-25 bombers, 30 P-51 Mustang fighters, 25 transport planes, 100 light aircraft, 150 gliders, and even 4 helicopters for Wingate's efforts, a virtual private air force commanded by Colonel Philip Cochran, model for Colonel Flip Corkin in the ever-present *Terry and the Pirates* comic strip that had inspired and then reflected so much American behavior earlier in the war.

The Chindits, as Wingate's raiders were called, had an RAF pilot on the ground with each column, coordinating these vital air drops. One of them was Terence O'Brien, who had taken part in the air defense of Singapore and was to write about it in *Chasing After Danger*. In his book about the

Wingate experience, *Out of the Blue: A Pilot with the Chindits* (1984), O'Brien describes what the General brought to the campaign in terms of both color and its effects:

> Our theatre of war had been starved for good news, and the fact that this first expedition had cost hundreds of lives for no direct military benefit was irrelevant against the powerful psychological boost it had given our forces; all the talk about Japanese mastery of jungle warfare, it was suggested, had now been proved unfounded by the march of Wingate's brigade right through the enemy lines into Burma and out again. In effect, its major achievement was to spotlight Wingate. He was carried on the crest of the publicity wave not only to London but thence onwards to the Quebec conference so impressing both Churchill and Roosevelt with his personality and ideas that he was given practically all he wanted—at the moment. His wants became wildly excessive, delirious perhaps, later on; but although his imperious manner and grandiose plans antagonized many of the staff at Delhi we in the columns certainly benefitted materially when he rocketed to stardom. Special equipment and rations began to pour in for us. The title of Special Forces began to have practical benefits as well as those for morale. (p. 21)

The parallels with Chennault are obvious, from the first good news in the face of presumed Japanese superiority to the swashbuckling methodology and its success with both the media and political leaders. But there was only one Wingate and just a few thousand of his raiders. Overall, British efforts in the Far East remained a much more deliberate affair.

One other way the RAF developed new methods was in clandestine operations. Here, too, Terence O'Brien played a role, flying the many such missions over Burma, Siam, Laos, and French Indo-China that form the narrative of his *The Moonlight War*. "Ours was the only theatre of the war in which four-engined aircraft did more parachute-dropping than bombing" (p. 62), he notes, and the distinction between who was covertly aiding who made for a fateful contrast. British forces flew American-made Liberators, ironically named, because the people they dropped and forces they supplied were, in the case of Indo-China, Gaullist French; the American Office of Strategic Services, at times using the

British-built Mosquito for its quick intrusions, preferred to help the Vietnamese directly, including a favorite named Ho Chi Minh. Nine years later some of these same OSS (now CIA) stations would be involved with sending in Chennault's pilots to help the French hold off Ho's forces for a time at Dien Bien Phu.

Hence, it was a colorful war, one for adventurers on all sides, few of whom fought by established rules of strategy. When it came to the Far East's war in the air, conduct was even more atypical, with revolutionary fighter doctrines developed by Chennault's AVG at the beginning and new emphases on ground attack, air supply, and clandestine operations. It was a style of air warfare that began in comic strips, flourished on the cover of *Life* magazine, and did not end until the last helicopter lifted off from the American Embassy's roof in Saigon a world later. At the time, an old AVG veteran named Charlie Bond was just beginning to enjoy his retirement as a major general in the United States Air Force, a career in which his penultimate posting had been in Thailand during the Vietnam War. "The chief stated that he chose me to represent the Air Force in Thailand because of my background and experience with American diplomats and foreign military officials, noting that I had been in the Orient with Chennault," Bond recalls in *A Flying Tiger's Diary*. "Leaving his office, I wondered if after twenty-five years my days with the Flying Tigers were still influencing my career" (p. 221).

They certainly were, just as Chennault's efforts with the AVG and on through the 1950s with CAT were influencing the war in Vietnam itself. During his eighteen months in this old theater for an even radically newer style of war, Charlie Bond would fly over airfields he'd bombed as a Flying Tiger, including the infamous target at Cheng Mai that inspired the AVG pilots' revolt. Although he never flew over China, he was certainly within range of where his old AVG colleague Erik Shilling had crash-landed on a hillside and been so terrified by the inquisitive mountain tribespeople reminiscent of threatening creatures from *Terry and the Pirates*.

Shilling's brief adventure with those tribesmen serves as

an apt encapsulation of the war that wasn't first. His P-40, just five years beyond being a state of the art example of what modern technology could produce, had fallen into a lost corner of the world where life was still in the Stone Age. If Shilling was off base by thinking these people were from a comic strip, they themselves were even more confused, believing this stranger who dropped from the skies was a visitor from outer space. In a circumstance as suggestive as anything in *A Connecticut Yankee in King Arthur's Court*, Erik Shilling could have done many things to amaze his hosts, albeit that he feared for his life. Because he was transporting personal gear on this mission, he was able to retrieve his wind-up gramophone from the crashed fuselage and for hours entertain these primitive people with the marvel of jazz records, to which they listened with rapt attention. As much as the Far East changed as a result of what began happening in 1941, this tiny hillside area was even more so never the same again.

Bibliography

Alsop, Joseph W., with Adam Platt. *"I've Seen the Best of It": Memoirs*. New York: Norton, 1992.

Beachamp, Gerry. *Mohawks over Burma*. Leicester: Midland Counties, 1985.

Bond, Charles R., Jr. *A Flying Tiger's Journey*. College Station: Texas A & M University Press, 1984.

Boyington, Gregory. *Baa Baa Black Sheep*. New York: Putnam, 1958.

———. *Tonya*. Indianapolis: Bobbs-Merrill, 1960.

Chennault, Anna. *A Thousand Springs: The Biography of a Marriage*. New York: Eriksson, 1962.

Chennault, Claire Lee. *Way of a Fighter*. New York: Putnam, 1949.

Cornelius, Wanda, and Thane Short. *Ding Hao: America's Air War in China, 1937-1945*. Gretna, La.: Pelican, 1980.

Cotton, M.C. "Bush." *Hurricanes over Burma*. London: Grub Street, 1995.

Donahue, Arthur Gerald. *Last Flight from Singapore*. New York: Macmillan, 1943.

———. *Tally-Ho! Yankee in a Spitfire*. New York: Macmillan, 1941.

Ford, Daniel. *Flying Tigers: Claire Chennault and the American Volunteer Group*. Washington, D.C.: Smithsonian Institution Press, 1991.

Frillmann, Paul, and Graham Peck. *China: The Remembered Life*. Boston: Houghton Mifflin, 1968.

Goodson, James A. *Tumult in the Clouds*. New York: St. Martin's, 1983.

Greenlaw, Olga S. *The Lady and the Tigers*. New York: Dutton, 1943.

Hemingway, Kenneth. *Wings over Burma*. London: Quality, 1944.

Hotz, Robert B., with George L. Paxton, Robert H. Neale, and Parker

S. Dupouy. *With General Chennault: The Story of the Flying Tigers.* New York: Coward-McCann, 1943.

Howard, James H. *Roar of the Tiger.* New York: Orion, 1991.

Innes, David J. *Beaufighters over Burma.* Poole: Blandford, 1985.

Kelly, Terence. *Hurricane and Spitfire Pilots at War.* London: William Kimber, 1986.

———. *Hurricane in Sumatra.* London: Arrow, 1991.

———. *Hurricane over the Jungle.* London: William Kimber, 1977.

Kent, J.A. *One of the Few.* London: William Kimber, 1971.

Klinkowitz, Jerome. *Their Finest Hours: Narratives of the RAF and Luftwaffe in World War II.* Ames: Iowa State University Press, 1989.

———. *Yanks over Europe: American Flyers in World War II.* Lexington: University Press of Kentucky, 1996.

Leonard, Royal. *I Flew for China.* Garden City, N.Y.: Doubleday, 1942.

Lopez, Donald S. *Into the Teeth of the Tiger.* New York: Bantam, 1986.

Losonsky, Frank S., and Terry M. Losonsky. *Flying Tiger: A Crew Chief's Story.* Atglen, Penn.: Schiffer, 1996.

Miller, Milt. *Tiger Tales.* Manhattan, Ks.: Sunflower University Press, 1984.

Molesworth, Carl. *Sharks over China: The 23rd Fighter Group in World War II.* Washington, D.C.: Brassey's, 1994.

———. *Wing to Wing.* New York: Orion, 1990.

Monks, Noel. *Squadrons Up!* London: Gollancz, 1940.

Neumann, Gerhard. *Herman the German.* New York: Morrow, 1984.

O'Brien, Terence. *Chasing After Danger.* London: William Collins, 1990.

———. *The Moonlight War.* London: William Collins, 1987.

———. *Out of the Blue: A Pilot with the Chindits.* London: William Collins, 1984.

Perrett, Geoffrey. *Winged Victory: The Army Air Forces in World War II.* New York: Random House, 1993.

Probert, Henry. *The Forgotten Air Force.* London: Brassey's, 1995.

Schultz, Duane. *The Maverick War.* New York: St. Martin's, 1987.

Scott, Robert Lee, Jr. *Damned to Glory.* New York: Scribner's, 1944.

———. *The Day I Owned the Sky.* New York: Bantam, 1988.

———. *Flying Tiger: Chennault of China.* Garden City, N.Y.: Doubleday, 1959.

———. *God Is My Co-Pilot.* New York: Scribner's, 1943.

Sevareid, Eric. *Not So Wild a Dream.* New York: Knopf, 1946.

Shores, Christopher, and Brian Cull, with Yashuo Izawa. *Bloody Shambles.* 2 vols. London: Grub Street, 1992 and 1993.

Shilling, Erik. *Destiny: A Flying Tiger's Rendezvous with Fate.* Privately printed, 1993.

Slessor, John. *The Central Blue.* London: Cassell, 1956.

Smith, Felix. *China Pilot: Flying for Chiang and Chennault.* Washington, D.C.: Brassey's, 1995.

Smith, Robert M. *With Chennault in China: A Flying Tiger's Diary*. Blue
      Ridge Summit, Penn.: TAB, 1984.
Smith, Robert T. *Tale of a Tiger*. Van Nuys, Calif.: Tiger Originals, 1986.
Sutton, Barry. *Jungle Pilot*. London: Macmillan, 1946.
————. *The Way of a Pilot*. London: Macmillan, 1942.
Whelan, Russell. *The Flying Tigers*. New York: Viking, 1942.

Index